TIM CLISSOLD studied Physics and Theoretical Physics at Cambridge University before moving to China and studying Mandarin Chinese. In the early 1990's, he co-founded a business that invested over four hundred million dollars in China. His first book, *Mr China*, was called 'an instant classic' by *Time Magazine* and was translated into fourteen languages. He then co-founded a second business that originated carbon offsets in China and currently runs another involved in dispute resolution.

祈立天，曾在剑桥大学学习物理和理论物理，后移居中国，学习中文。20世纪90年代初期，他参与了一项投资，在中国投资四亿多美元。祈立天出版的第一本书《中国通》(*Mr China*) 被《时代周刊》誉为"即时经典之作"，并被译为十四种语言。后来，祈立天又在中国参与创立了一个二氧化碳减排基金。目前，祈立天经营的公司负责处理争端解决事宜。

Cloud
Chamber

云室

一个英国人眼中的中国古诗

〔英〕祈立天(Tim Clissold) 著译

徐懿春 译(前言)

创于1897　商务印书馆
The Commercial Press

图书在版编目(CIP)数据

云室:一个英国人眼中的中国古诗:汉、英/(英)祈立天
著译;徐懿春译.—北京:商务印书馆,2022(2023.7 重印)
ISBN 978 - 7 - 100 - 20436 - 1

Ⅰ.①云…　Ⅱ.①祈… ②徐…　Ⅲ.①古典诗歌—
诗歌研究—中国—汉、英　Ⅳ.①I207.2

中国版本图书馆 CIP 数据核字(2021)第 208625 号

云室

——一个英国人眼中的中国古诗

〔英〕祈立天　著译

徐懿春　译(前言)

商 务 印 书 馆 出 版
(北京王府井大街36号　邮政编码100710)
商 务 印 书 馆 发 行
北京中科印刷有限公司印刷
ISBN 978 - 7 - 100 - 20436 - 1

2022 年 1 月第 1 版　　　　开本 880×1240　1/32
2023 年 7 月北京第 3 次印刷　印张 12⅜

定价:98.00 元

for
my mother
Rachel Mary

但愿长醉不复醒
古来圣贤皆寂寞
惟有饮者留其名

主人何为言少钱
径须沽取对君酌
五花马　千金裘
呼儿将出换美酒
与尔同销万古愁
　　　　李白

How many thinkers have been forgotten through the ages?
Great drinkers are remembered more than sober sages;
I only want to drink and never wake up.

How can our host complain about money?
Just fetch another barrel at once.
His horse with the plaited mane!
His furs of a thousand gold pieces!
Call the boy and have him swap them for fine wine and
　　together you and I will wipe out the cares of ten thousand years.

Li Bai

701–762 CE

目　录
CONTENTS

Introduction / 前言

Poems / 诗歌

【 上 ∣ Up 】

【 下 | Down 】

【 奇 | Strangeness 】

【 魅 | Charm 】

5

Contents 目录

【 美 | Beauty 】

【 真 | Truth 】

城南上原陈翁，以卖花为业，得钱悉供酒资；又不能

独饮，逢人辄强与共醉。辛亥九月十二日，偶过其门，访

7

Contents 目 录

Translation of Introduction / 前言译文
（后起）

9

Contents　目　录

Introduction

前言

1
Origin and Acknowledgement

That year, it just rained and rained. It poured through the autumn and pelted defiantly on into winter. It bucketed for weeks on end with such single-minded determination that I feared my house might flood.

Having recently moved, I was new to the immediate surroundings. Friends had warned me against buying a place on the banks of a river in the age of climate change but I had fallen for the little stone-roofed cottage and the ruined twelfth century abbey close by. After I noticed a family of ducks swimming past my window and across what I had only recently assumed was a flowerbed, I assembled a defensive line of sandbags drawn up in solemn rows around the door. In the end, the waters relented after the first few splashes on the doorstep. I felt lucky. I heard that there was a village in Wales where it had rained every day for eighty-four days; I wondered how anyone could stand it. And, feeling rather soggy myself, and also quite behind in organising festivities that year, I hurriedly sent cards to my friends and threw in a verse written a thousand years ago by a Chinese poet named Su Shi, which seemed quite apt both for the season and the new lodgings.

> *This year again the rain is exhausting,*
> *months of dreary autumn-like weather.*
> *Lying in bed, I listen to the showers on the crab-apple blossom*
> *their petals fall down to the mire.*

> *The Spring river wants to pour through my window,*
> *the force of the rain is unrelenting.*
> *My small house is like a little fishing boat*
> *amid a fog of clouds and water.*
> *In an empty kitchen I boil cold vegetables,*
> *in a broken stove I burn wet weeds.*
> *How would I know that today is the Cold-food Festival*
> *if it wasn't for the ravens with paper money in their beaks?*

I was surprised by the response and the interest my friends showed towards the lines, so over the following months as the world's northern axis tilted towards the sun, I searched for verses on brighter seasons. And the more I dug into Chinese poetry, the more I was struck by the contemporary relevance of the ancient lines. Our own daily headlines jumped from the page despite the distance in time and space.

One of China's greatest poets—writing twelve hundred years ago—was a refugee from war. From the very first lines, I could picture him instantly as a gaunt and troubled figure standing on the walls of a ransacked city, looking over a landscape ravaged by war and desperate for news from home. I went further. I found other poets fixated with social injustices—homelessness, uneven wealth distribution, tax evasion, even food banks. Elsewhere, there were verses about the indignities of old age—baldness, losing one's teeth—of end-of-life dilemmas. Another wrote of the damage caused to the environment by unrestrained exploitation of natural resources, such as unsustainable logging or the effect on the food-chain of the removal of predators. It felt as if 'Gaia Theory' had come echoing down ten centuries. Elsewhere poets grieve over infant mortality or fret about social mobility. I sensed a trace of substance abuse and bipolar disorder in the spontaneity of the eighth century poets, as they drank themselves into a state of utter leglessness, only to rise up suddenly in a frenzy, grab their writing brushes and sweep great swathes of indecipherable characters across the walls, the ceilings, the floors, the furniture. It sounded like a medieval rave. Then I read about the Crow Terrace Trial in 1079, where a poet was exiled after a robust defence of free speech. Gradually, I built an outline picture of the poets in the Tang and the Song dynasties and started translating their words; and this is what I found—

Chinese poetry constitutes a vast civilizational asset. It is the most extensive body of coherent literature of any culture at any time. It consists of tens of thousands—possibly hundreds of thousands—of poems running in an unbroken chain from the

6

twenty-third century BC until the present day. It is distinct from our own, and yet ideas and feelings overlap. Its sentiments are universal, yet the mode of expression unique. Poetry occupies a central position in Chinese society; people here quote it for enjoyment all the time. For generations, poetry has infected the imaginations, ambitions, desires, and the hopes of Chinese men and women more profoundly than any other branch of their culture. It encapsulates the innermost beliefs and feelings of the beating Chinese heart—and by doing that, it has shaped the present day manifestation of this great and ancient civilisation. It is the defining cultural inspiration that has worked its way into the DNA of the whole of the Chinese people. To appreciate the ideas behind Chinese poetry is to find a window onto the mind of contemporary China.

In this book, I have chosen poems which convey feelings that come up in daily life in China rather than trying to produce an anthology that seeks to represent a balanced overview of the whole genre. Like plenty of others before me, as I marvelled at the lines shining across a thousand years, I wanted to bring them to a wider audience so that one day Chinese poems might be regarded as the common property of the whole of humanity and not—as in the West—just the province of a few specialists. But I have another motive too for the more practically minded. As China moves back towards centre stage in that ceaselessly shifting world order, it has started to affect the lives of millions beyond its own borders. For those who want to maintain a voice in this unfolding narrative, it is surely advantageous to understand the patterns of Chinese thought. I want to explain how knowledge of these poems can give a direct operational advantage to any foreigner dealing with China either at home or abroad.

Where they are available, I have been guided at difficult junctures by translations of the poems—but I have always worked from the original. There are marvellous and inspirational translations out there, from scholars such as Tony Barnstone, Chou Ping, David Hinton, Perry Link, Stephen Owen, Bill Porter, Kenneth Rexroth and the late, great pioneer Arthur Waley. I salute them all, and it's an honour to sit at the feet of these Masters.

I would like to thank James Kynge for introducing me to Chinese poetry in the first place, Carrie Gracie for ploughing through an early draft, and Jo and Alistair Michie for insisting that I wrote about it and their limitless supplies of gin. Jim O'Neil, Nicholas Barber, Andrew Methven and Freda Merck gave wonderful commentaries that made me stand back and look at wider vistas. Xinran painted the broad arc of Chinese poetry and explained the more difficult parts to me. I also want to thank Dorothy Clague for lending me her precious collection of Chinese poetry books—and not worrying too much when I thought I'd lost them—and Nicky Hansell for her unflagging interest, support and goodwill. I want to acknowledge the debt of gratitude that I owe to my great friend and colleague Frank Li, who has for many years patiently and carefully explained key aspects of China's culture and history to me. I also want to express my appreciation and admiration to my brilliant but modest translator, Rose Xu, who

Introduction 前言

was so industrious that she made sense of my writing, even when it was confused in the English original. I would also like to thank the team at The Commercial Press, Ma Haolan and Guo Chaofeng, and my exceptionally diligent editor Du Maoli. Finally, I want to thank Jenny Lawrence from the bottom of my heart, whose tireless encouragement has meant so much to me as a writer.

This book was first published by The Commercial Press of China, so the initial audience was Chinese. If a Chinese author wrote a book about Shakespeare, we would probably not read it to deepen our understanding of his work. But we might read it to understand the journey the Chinese author had taken and the difficulties she or he encountered. We would have been there to suffer the slings and arrows of outrageous fortune, or perhaps to take arms against a sea of troubles; we might have chuckled together at the sevens ages of man, with the 'lean and slippered pantaloon.' But above all, at the end, when all was said and done, we would have taken a step back, joined hands and, in silence, marvelled at the universal truths that Shakespeare revealed about the shape of a human life. These poets do that too.

Tim Clissold

惊蛰，2021

$$\sigma_x \sigma_p \geq \frac{\hbar}{2}$$

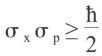

Heisenberg's Uncertainty Principle
海森堡的不确定性原理

9

Introduction　前言

2
Heisenberg's Uncertainty

The Chinese have always struck me as being thoroughly at ease with uncertainty. Conversely, in the West, there's—what shall we say?—a certain queasiness with ambiguity; a need to know what will happen; a desire to explain rather than just to accept; the longing for a clear end to a story. For at least three centuries, Western science has been on a quest for precision in its description of the world around us. Ironically, this search for the perfect explanation ended up with Heisenberg. When, in 1927, he came up with his famous 'Uncertainty Principle,' he laid the foundations of modern physics and revolutionised scientific thinking. But at the same time he placed an absolute limit on what is knowable. Einstein never liked it and remarked grumpily: 'God doesn't play dice with the universe.'

Personally, I don't think God plays dice at all. He's far too busy. But with the short inequality on the last page, Heisenberg changed the meaning of reality. Waves became particles; particles became waves. The universe collapsed into a set of probability distributions. The long search for perfect order, a quest that had marched triumphantly across and then down the columns of the periodic table and used calculus to set the planets singing harmonically in their orbits, orbits described perfectly—or, as it turned out, not quite so perfectly—by Newtonian mechanics, eventually bumped up against its own limits. When Heisenberg wove uncertainty into the fabric of space-time, he shook Western assumptions about the knowable; but at the same time, he came up with an idea that sits much more comfortably with the Chinese. For they—several thousand years earlier—had knitted ambiguity into the very threads of their own language.

3
Uncertainty in Chinese

The title of Heisenberg's original paper[1] contains a word that cannot be translated exactly into English; I sincerely hope that was deliberate. I am told on good authority that, '*anschaulichen*' is one of those German words that defy an unambiguous translation.

Heisenberg's chosen word has been variously translated as '*physical,*' '*perceptible*' and '*perceptual.*' I remember vaguely reading somewhere that the closest literal translation of '*anschaulichen*' is 'visualizable' but it is, I think, rather satisfying that no one is sure enough to take a stand on it. Whilst ambiguity should be expected when moving from one language into another, such as German to English, a whole new world of kaleidoscopic confusion and chaos appears in mesmerizing technicolour when there is uncertainty within one language, rather than just across two.

In Chinese, imprecision is part of daily life. People are inured

---

1 "Ueber den anschaulichen Inhalt der quantentheoretischen Kinematik und Mechanik"

to it in a way that would infuriate lawyers, quantity surveyors and actuaries everywhere else. There's a vagueness about everyday language and thought that just accepts the observable without needing to explain it; for example, Chinese medicine, as a friend once remarked drily, can't really be explained scientifically, but "it tells you roughly how to live, whereas Western medicine tells you exactly how you'll die. " [1]

Chinese grammar, in comparison with say German or Hungarian, borders on the non-existent. Verbs, for example, remain unchanged in different phases of time, *viz.*:

> Today I eat pickled cabbage for breakfast;
> Yesterday I eat pickled cabbage for breakfast;
> Tomorrow I eat pickled cabbage for breakfast!

Things that have long been extinct in our own language remain alive in Chinese, so that:

> 'Genghis Khan <u>was</u> a very nice chap,'
> and
> 'Genghis Khan <u>is</u> a very nice chap'

are indistinguishable in Chinese. Without separation in

---

1 中医让你糊里糊涂地活，
西医让你明明白白地死。

language or thought between 'what is' and 'what was,' China's past seems to merge into its present.

Nouns and pronouns do not change to indicate case or number, nor do they exhibit gender. [1] 'One book, two book, three book, four'—'she give he three book' or 'she give she three book,' or even 'he give he three book,' who the hell knows? You end up wondering if it was the book that gave him to her.

There is no definite or indefinite article. Traditionally, there was no punctuation, no nominative, accusative, dative, genitive or ablative with which to humiliate the ponderous schoolboy, just a chain of ideas and a lexicon of characters large enough to boggle the mind. Fifty-three thousand, I'm told, at least. [2]

Uncertainty in the spoken word is compounded by the extensive occurrence of homophones, which are words that sound exactly the same or are so confusingly similar that it makes your brain ache and sends cramps coursing up your tongue. In my pocket dictionary, there are more than fifty words all pronounced '*shi*,' meaning—to choose just a small selection—'lion,' 'louse,' 'persimmon,' 'alpine yarrow,' the element 'cerium,' 'excrement,' 'corpse,' 'poem' and 'a horizontal bar used in the front of a chariot as an armrest.' No wonder the pages are worn so thin with desperate fumbling. And—yes, yes—of course, I hear

---

1   '*Ta*' can mean 'he,' 'she' or 'it,' although I admit that the characters are distinct.

2   According to the *Zhonghua Dacidian*.

the Chinese speakers amongst you point out that some of those seemingly identical words are distinguished by one of the four different tones that inflect the spoken word. But I would press the point and say that, for example, there are more than twenty different characters all identically pronounced '*shū*,' using the raised first tone, with meanings including variously 'book,' 'comb,' 'uncle,' 'beans,' 'vegetables,' 'foot,' 'hemp,' 'door hinge' and 'an ancient weapon made of bamboo.' [1]

As a result, one has to go to great lengths to define a word taken out of context or where there is no context given. For example, it would be completely unremarkable to shake hands with a Chinese person and hear them say "Hello, I'm Section Chief *Zhāng*, that's the character *Zhāng* made out of a 'bow' and 'eternal'" or "I'm Vice-Mayor *Wáng*, that's the *Wáng* that means 'boundless oceans' not the one that means 'king.'" So I think, however much you may argue to the contrary, there's a good case to say that without further explanation, a character lacking a clear context is often difficult and sometimes impossible to identify with certainty if one relies purely on the sound.

Once, a friend ordered some boiled water in a restaurant. But the waitress hesitated. There is no tense in Chinese; I could sense her wondering if he meant 'boiling water' or 'boiled water.' So he expanded: 'Cold, boiled water!' That made it worse. She looked

---

1   There are four tones in spoken Mandarin Chinese (i) *pāi* or 'high-level,' (ii) *pái* or 'rising,' (iii) *pǎi* or 'falling then rising' and (iv) *pài* or 'falling.'

completely blank. I could see the concept of cold boiling water slowly developing in her mind. So he took a step back and gave the full explanation:

'Please can I have some water that was originally cold and that was then boiled and then left to cool down again so that I can be sure that it is clean.'

'Yes,' she said without the slightest change in expression.

But there was a further complication. He had used the expression '*liáng de kāi shuǐ*,' meaning 'cold boiled water' which sounds almost identical to '*liǎng ge kāi shuǐ*,' meaning 'two cups of boiling water.' So there had to be another round of negotiations before everything was finally settled and we could all relax. [1]

Another time in a hotel, a friend called down to complain that the sheets were dirty, only to find a maid at the door a few minutes later with a tray of clean glasses. '*Bèizi*' (falling tone) means 'sheets,' whereas '*bēizi*' (raised flat tone) means 'cups.' '*Yán*' means 'salt' whilst '*yān*' means 'tobacco.' And so it goes on. '*Tiānxià*' means 'China' or—revealingly— 'the whole world' depending on what you are getting at. '*Tuǒxié*' means 'compromise' but '*tuōxié*' means 'slippers.' When I don't have enough to do, I like to imagine some visiting businessmen banging the table at a contract negotiation and shouting

---

1 I should apologise for having told this anecdote elsewhere, but I must confess that I could not think of another that relayed the point as clearly.

furiously, 'We've made hundreds of slippers and now it's time for you to make some too.' I doubt the Chinese would bat an eyelid. Finally, '*ǎo*' meaning 'kind old lady' should never be confused with '*áo*' meaning 'a huge legendary turtle.' [1]

The written language can be equally confusing. For instance, 己, 已 and 巳 are all completely different characters meaning '*jǐ*'—'self'—'*yǐ*'—'already'—and '*sì*'—the sixth 'Heavenly Stem,' which itself would need a short essay to describe properly. 李, 季 and 孝 aren't much better;[2] nor are 休 and 体. 蜜蜂 means 'bee,' whereas if you reverse the characters 蜂蜜 they become 'honey.' I can never remember which is which.

An additional concept in the written language is a 'radical,' which combines with other vaguely phonetic elements to form a full character. These radicals, many of which do not have actual meaning themselves, imply a general quality to the full character. 氵 for example, implies 'water,' through the image of three drops of said substance. Thus 湖—lake—江—river—港—harbour—滩—beach. 扌 means 'hand' or 'grasp,' 犭 means 'dog' or 'animal' whilst 宀 means roof. But none of these radicals can appear in isolation; they are meaningful only in combination with other character elements, bound up with other

Introduction 前言

---

1 Even more alarmingly, the characters 鰶 and 痔 both pronounced '*zhì*' with a falling tone mean respectively 'sardines' and 'haemorrhoids.'

2 They mean 'plum,' 'season' and 'filial piety' respectively, as you would expect.

parts to form a greater whole.

Thus, '*píng*' 平, a character in its own right, meaning 'balanced,' 'flat' or 'unruffled' will combine with radicals to form other characters, each with different meanings. 平 is visually quite balanced and unruffled, don't you think? Combined with 'fish,' 鱼 it becomes '*píng*' 鲆 meaning a 'flat fish,' such as a plaice. Combined with 'earth,' 土 it becomes '*píng*' 坪 meaning 'a flat raised terrace.' With 'wood,' 木 it becomes '*píng*' 枰, meaning a flat wooden object, such as a chessboard or wooden bed; it all seems quite logical so far. Combined with the water and grass radicals, respectively 氵and ⺿ it becomes '*píng*' 萍 meaning 'duckweed,' which floats on the top of an unruffled pond. And with 'mouth,' 口 it becomes '*píng*' 呯, the sound of a 'short bang' or indeed a '*ping*!' But predictably this apparent order soon breaks down in as the '*píng*'s 胼 and 蚲 mean, respectively 'fatty or oily' [1] and 'earthworm' neither of which—particularly the 'earthworm'—can be considered as especially 'flat,' unless, I suppose, someone had stood on it. Thus one can often guess at a meaning from the radical and the sound from the phonetic, such as in the various '*píng*'s above, but never with sufficient reliability to make it really worth the effort.

---

1 This character also has a second pronunciation '*pēng*,' when it means 'abdominal distension,' thereby promptly causing said affliction by reminding language students of the truly appalling fact that some characters have more than one pronunciation.

It gets worse. Sometimes even the same character has multiple and potentially contradictory meanings. '*Hèn*' — 恨 — for example, means both 'hate' and 'regret,' which are really quite different, don't you think? The character 苍 is defined in one dictionary as meaning grey-green, greenish-blue, grey-black <u>and</u> silvery-white[1] and 须臾 as both 'momentarily' and 'at length,' which appear to me to be opposites. 抚 can mean 'to caress' and 'to slap,' two actions that seem quite distinct to me.[2] The meanings can sometimes be so diverse that it is almost impossible to be certain which one to use. A project to compile a comprehensive Chinese-English dictionary[3] was abandoned in 1955 after the first print run contained 68 double-columned pages just to define the single character 子. Other characters have no meaning at all. They are just included to preserve rhythm or indicate some obscure link between others.

Even when the Chinese language does provide precision, it seems to do it in a way that invites incredulity, as the sheer degree of specificity makes the words almost impossible to use. There is, for example, a word for 'driving a cart across a field in a north-

Introduction 前言

---

1 苍 means the colour of distantly indistinct mountains blurred through a haze, I think, but it's rather difficult to tell since when combined with the character 黄, meaning 'yellow,' it also seems to mean 'to turn upside down or inside out' and 'shocked and startled.'

2 But are they? Stroke, as in 'six strokes' (with a cane) and stroke, as in 'he stroked the cat' (presumably not with a cane).

3 The Harvard-Yenching Institute project.

south direction' and a completely different one to drive it from east to west. '*E*'—咢—means 'to beat a drum with one's hand but not sing.' Elsewhere, the word 箕裘—*jīqiú*—is defined in one dictionary as meaning 'the art of making sieves and fur coats.'[1] Sieves and fur coats, one murmurs to oneself. Where did that come from? Another, 轼[2], is defined elsewhere as 'to salute with a half-bow whilst riding in a carriage or chariot.' Finally, I came across a word that described 'any object that, from a distance, looks like a swarm of insects.'[3] I was quite annoyed when I later found out that this word originated from a fictional work called the *Celestial Emporium of Benevolent Knowledge*, and that it is not, in fact, a Chinese word. But at least it proves that I am not the only one intrigued by these bizarre granules of specificity in the Chinese language, lodged, as they are, in a miasma of confusion.

Beyond the meaning of individual words, the Chinese appear comfortable with whole sentences of almost psychedelic ambiguity. Perhaps there is some peace to be found away from the complexities of life in the refuge of the unsaid, the imprecise and the vague—

---

1 www. chinese-dictionary. org

2 This is the same character as the name of one of the famous poets, Su Shi.

3 It was included in a fictional taxonomy of creatures, which included (i) those that belong to the emperor, (ii) embalmed ones, (iii) those that are trained, (iv) suckling pigs, (v) mermaids, (vi) fabulous ones, (vii) stray dogs, (viii) those that tremble as if they were mad and (ix) those drawn with a very fine camel hair brush.

who could possibly tell?[1]

An example, if I may: I was once involved in a dispute with a Chinese business partner over control of a factory which left several people in hospital. The conflict broke out after we had spent three years trying to install a financial controller to look after our money, and, after being thwarted at every turn, we stumbled across a major fraud. In the midst of the crisis, I heard that the Party Secretary, who was the top leader in the city, was having dinner at a local hotel, so I went over and waited outside the room where he was carousing with his colleagues. Surprisingly, he agreed to see me.

At the meeting, on advice from my Chinese colleagues, I avoided the direct approach and opted for Chinese obliqueness. In describing the fraud, I used the phrase '*zīchǎn guǎnlǐ quèshí yǒu wèntí*'—or 'the assets management indeed has problems.' He replied without missing a heartbeat '*shì chū yǒu yīn*'—or 'when something happens there might be a reason.' If one was bold enough to translate that exchange more directly into English, then I would say that 'the assets management indeed has problems' really meant 'those bastards have just stolen eight million quid from us, and your officials have done bugger all about it!' And

Introduction 前言

---

1 I once asked a Chinese friend whether the characters '最喜小儿' in line 7 of Xin Qiji's poem on page 200 meant 'favourite boy' or 'happiest boy' and he just asked me why I thought it mattered, since the happiest one was probably also the most popular.

his reply, 'when something happens there might be a reason' would be more accurately translated to 'well, if you're so stupid to invest all that money here and never send an accountant, what the fuck did you expect?!'

4

Echoes from the Eighth Century

If we move beyond everyday language, where—as we agreed earlier—the imprecision would enrage accountants and loss adjusters everywhere, when it comes to poetry, it gives the reader space.

Chinese poems achieve movement without verbs, images without adjectives, personality without pronouns. Whilst it can be said that all art—and poetry and literature in particular—is in some senses 'a translation' because it is viewed through the prism of the reader's individual experiences, assumptions and desires, the vagueness in Chinese poetry allows scope for the imagination in entirely different dimensions. 花非花，雾非雾，meaning 'a flower that is no flower, in fog that is not fog,' was written by one of China's greatest poets in a rare burst of candour more than a thousand years ago.[1] In those six characters, as someone once said wistfully, 'who can discern the contours of the original stone that lie behind the curtain of our memories?' [2]

---

1 Or was it candour? I am suspicious that he was, in fact, describing his lover's vagina.

2 It was Adam Williams in *Portrait of a City*.

So, when it comes to translating Chinese poems, an aspiring but inexperienced novice—like me—will inevitably stub his or her proverbial toe painfully against seven specific, immovable and rather jagged rocks:

Subjectlessness: it is the norm in classical Chinese poetry to omit subjects. As in modern-day text messages, the reader must infer the actor in the scene—邮件看到了 — 'email seen'— but by whom? Whilst this vagueness is normal for us all in simple messages texted on the hoof or running for a taxi—and indeed the meaning is obvious because of context—the complexity expands exponentially when applied to more subtle ideas in poetry.

In the first line of a famous poem, which is composed of the five characters 'empty mountain not see person,' no one would say that 'empty mountain' should be the subject just because it is a noun and comes first. Common sense infers the subject to be an unstated human viewer. But how can one put this effect into Western languages that insist that subjects be stated? If 'I' is inserted, it introduces the mind of the poet and destroys the effect of something just happening without anyone necessarily being there to see it.

Numberlessness: nouns, as we have seen, have no number in Chinese. 'A rose is a rose is a roses,' but actually of course they aren't (or isn't). It's just a sort of rosiness; like 'tableness' hovering around a table. Tableness, I think you'd agree, is not the summation of individual tables—like at wedding that you really didn't want to go to—it's just the attributes of being a table, right? So what should the translator do? 'Tableness' sounds weird and 'tablehood' is ridiculous but that's sort of what the Chinese means.

Tenselessness: there are several ways in Chinese to specify when something happened or will happen—or indeed is going on right under your nose—but verb tense is not one of them. For poets, the great advantage of tenselessness is the ambiguity it opens up. Did I see no one in the hills? Or am I now seeing no one? Am I imagining what it would be like to see no one? Or is he, or she? Or they? All these, and others, are possible. The sun seems to rise on a landscape where the time is so vague that it could be the same as when it sets. The true meanings of these poems are like tiny particles, flying imperceptibly around in some quantum mechanical probability-space; we know they are there but we can never really see them clearly enough or observe them directly to be sure.

Assumption of knowledge: as in Renaissance painting, Chinese poems often assume a familiarity with obscure background knowledge. Criticism of those in power, for example, is often so veiled that normal people without several PhD's in 'Chinese Classical Idioms' would probably miss it. A poem seemingly about the majesty of an imperial hunt may actually be drawing attention to the vast slaughter of powerless animals as a parallel to the treatment of ordinary people by a despot. But the despot himself will only be hinted at by vague references to some historical literary event or personality because, naturally,

Introduction 前言

if the poet was clearer, then both he and his entire family would promptly be executed.

Particular flowers or animals represent various qualities; for example, chrysanthemums represent constancy or longevity because they continue to bloom on into autumn after others have withered; the lotus represents purity as its spotless flowers rise up from the mire. Mandarin ducks embody marital fidelity because they mate for life; geese show steadfastness of purpose as they fly in straight lines. They also symbolise respect for hierarchy by agreeing to fly in V-shaped formations and sometimes represent a traveller far from home due to their migrations. And so it goes on. Willows represent fickleness, frivolity—even prostitution—because they bend this way and that in the wind. Pines denote longevity and a person of upright principle because they refuse to change colour just for the seasons. Bamboo is loved by scholars for a similar reason—it stays green in the winter—but also because it springs back to the upright as soon as the storm has passed. Plum blossoms show fortitude as they blossom so early in the Spring. The wu'tong tree—*sterculia plantaniflora,* which defies consistent translation but is sometimes called the phoenix tree—represents heightened sensibility as its white, soft wood is perfect for making the musical instruments that give expression to the emotions of the musician. [1]

---

1 There are parallels, so I'm told, in the Western world where, for example, pomegranates represent fertility in ancient Greek verse due to their profusion of seeds.

Brevity: this vagueness is combined with a brevity—or perhaps more accurately high information density—that would be the envy of tabloid headline writers everywhere. There is a story that about a thousand years ago, as one of China's great poets waited outside the Hanlin Academy[1] with his associates, they witnessed an unusual event. A horse became spooked, galloped down a busy street, and kicked a dog to death that had been sleeping there. The poet challenged his two associates to express this event in writing. One wrote: 'A dog was lying in the thoroughfare and was kicked to death by a galloping horse,' while the other wrote: 'A horse galloped down a thoroughfare. A lying dog encountered it and was killed.' The poet mocked his junior colleagues, 'A history book in your hands would remain incomplete after ten thousand volumes,' he said. When asked for his own rendering, he replied serenely: 'Galloping horse killed dog in street' — '逸马杀犬于道.' But translating the poems into line after line of tabloid headlines would ruin them so it's difficult to know what to do.

Rhythm: whilst the meaning of the poems demonstrates ambiguity and deliberate flexibility, the structure on the other hand can be extremely rigid. Most of the poems here consist

---

1 The Hanlin Academy— 'Hanlin' means 'Forest of Writing Brushes'— was an elite academic and administrative council set up in the eighth century to review the classics, interpret them and set the guidelines for the civil service *ke-ju* exams, which are described later.

strictly of lines of five or seven characters. You will notice later that, as a result of this regularity, the poems often appear oblong on the page. This structure imparts a rhythm to the poems which impels them forward in a way that—due to the information density of each line—makes it almost impossible to capture in English.

Permutation: if one character has two meanings, that makes life difficult but bearable. If five characters in a row each have two meanings, the number of permutations for the overall meaning—you mathematicians will tell us—is 2^5. Unfortunately for the translator, this is 32.

If the number of meanings to each character is three, this number rises to 243. And if the number of characters in each line goes from five to seven, the equivalent figure is 2,187. But many characters have five or six meanings so, there isn't really much I can say—except to relate an example.

In the poem, 'Leaving Longbank Village' on page 193, the characters that constitute line 17 '五月不可触' have been translated by Kenneth Roxreth as:

'you should not risk the dangerous floods of May'

whereas

'I haven't touched you for five months,'

is the same line translated by Barnstone and Chou.

Each of these inspirational translators has provided remarkable and accurate insights into hundreds of poems; neither can be right or wrong. But we all crash up against the remorseless mathematics of permutation and we are forced to make our own choice in the end. [1] In fact, Burton Watson, the great translator of Chinese and Japanese poetry remarked rather kindly on one of the greatest Chinese poets, 'there are many different ways to approach the problems involved in translating Du Fu, which is why we need as many different translations as possible. '

1　My own version is: 'I have not been able to feel you for five long months 'til now' because I could not help but sense yearning in the poem—and I tried to catch its rhythm.

5

Quarks and Colour Confinement

Now, my friend, after that brief sojourn through the architecture of Chinese poetry—an architecture that you will agree at times seems to demonstrate alarming structural instability—I must ask for your indulgence as I pass briefly through the more difficult bits of this story.

You can indeed be forgiven for despairing, as we enter the world of subatomic particles. But please don't. If there are words here that are not familiar, ignore them and plough on. I can hardly understand them myself these days. Indeed, Wolfgang Pauli, one of the pioneers of quantum physics, who was nominated for a Nobel prize by Einstein himself, remarked of the bewildering number of subatomic particles, 'Had I foreseen this, I would have gone into botany instead. ' So you're in good company and I promise not to tarry here too long.

Let's start with the ancient Greeks. As early as the sixth century BC, they thought that matter existed as a collection of tiny particles. Fast-forward abruptly about twenty-five centuries to 1805, and we find a poor weaver who could not afford to educate his son; and we find that son, John Dalton, living in Manchester, and we see him striding up the peaks in the Lake District, first taking meteorological measurements and then later turning his mind towards the atom. Taking his queue from the ancient Greeks, he showed that each element is made up of distinct 'atoms,' or 'ἄτομος' meaning 'indivisible.'

Next came Mendeleev, struggling out of poverty in a small village in Siberia and dreaming of the gilded crosses atop the onion-domes of St Petersburg. There, in 1869, he organized each of Dalton's elements into the periodic table, bringing order out of nature's chaos and predicting several elements that had not then been discovered. He was—perhaps more significantly—also responsible for standardizing the content of alcohol in Russian vodka at forty percent. I would have gone for fifty.

Now that we've sorted out atoms, chemists can start building them into molecules. But if instead of following the chemists into that larger world of plastics, nylons and fertilisers (and who could resist it?) we follow the particle physicists into the subatomic world and peer into that inner realm, what do you think we might find inside the atom itself?

Electrons were discovered in 1896, when a New Zealander working at Cambridge showed that the atom might be split into even smaller parts, which carried electrical charge. Ten years later, when for some reason Rutherford started firing alpha particles at thin gold sheets, it became obvious that atoms consisted largely of empty space with a very small nucleus at the centre and electrons whizzing around it. A little later, when he smashed together two nitrogen atoms, Rutherford showed that the atomic nucleus contained protons. I think Rutherford enjoyed smashing things together.

Finally, in 1937, the son of a northern cotton spinner discovered the neutron. So together these three pioneering scientists—Thompson, Rutherford and Chadwick, all of whom worked at the Cavendish Laboratories in Cambridge—created the atomic model of matter. Their genius was to propose that the atom itself consisted of a positively charged nucleus made of protons and neutrons, with electrons somehow whirling around it in orbitals.

For the next step in the story, we have to peer out far into space, or—to be more specific—we have to look at the stream of high energy particles, or 'cosmic rays, ' that flow from far-off galaxies and into our own solar system. Astrophysicists are not yet sure of the origin of these cosmic rays, but there's a constellation up there called the 'Great Bear' or Ursa Major, which seems to be the source of particularly high energy rays. It may be something to do with exploding supernovas, the astrophysicists aren't sure; but whatever's going on out there, it's pretty bad, and you really don't want to get involved.

By using a 'cloud chamber[1],' a simple apparatus that can

1　A cloud chamber is a straightforward device used to detect the pathways of incoming cosmic ray particles by suddenly lowering the pressure of a saturated vapour so that the tracks of the particles cause droplets to condense

photograph the incoming tracks of these cosmic rays, scientists discovered a bewildering number of distinct elementary particles beyond those just found in atoms, each with different masses, charges and spins. Then, in October 1946 and May 1947, two unexpected events occurred that seemed to reveal previously unknown particles.

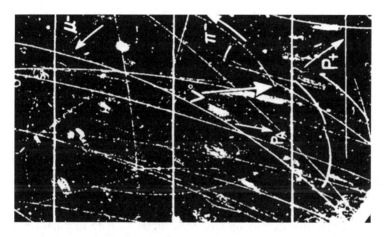

The researchers, who found the particles in Manchester, published the photograph above, which—you will all instantly recognize—clearly shows the track of something called a K-meson travelling across a cloud chamber. The scientists

(last page) out of the vapour. These droplets, which are nucleated by ionisation along the path of the incoming particle, can be photographed to reveal the 'track.' The properties of the particle can be investigated by applying electrical or magnetic fields to the cloud chamber and watching the effect that these have on the path of the particle. Cloud chambers were invented in 1911 by a Scottish meteorologist working on Ben Nevis and they played a key role in the discovery of subatomic particles in the 1930's and 40's, a process which eventually led to quark theory.

identified the track by a small white arrow, which one cannot help noticing is itself almost unidentifiable and mixed up with another four arrows that have been inserted seemingly in order to confuse the K-meson with other particles. Physicists, apparently, can never resist the opportunity for a joke.

According to accepted theory at the time, this K-meson particle should have decayed in ten trillion trillionths of a second. The lifetime observed in the photograph was actually a trillion times longer than expected. Scientists could not explain how the particle lasted so long, so they called the behavior 'strange.' Thus, strangeness became one of the basic ideas in elementary particle physics. Physicists started pondering the possibility that, in addition to mass, charge and magnetic spin—which are the basic properties observable to us in the human world—there could be other basic properties inherent in subatomic particles that do not manifest themselves directly to our senses, such as 'strangeness.'

As time went on, the experimenters discovered a large and ever-growing family of particles. They called this group of particles 'hadrons[1],' meaning 'stout ones,' and the group

---

1 'Hadron' comes from 'άδρός' or 'hadrós' meaning 'stout' or 'thick.' They turned out to be composite particles made of quarks held together by the strong force in a way that is somewhat analogous to a molecule but at the subatomic particle level. Hadrons are studied in colliders, such as the Large Hadron Collider, which consists of about 10,000 superconducting magnets cooled down to about -270°C and perfectly arranged in an underground, circular tunnel near Geneva that has a circumference of 27 kilometers. The Large Hadron Collider cost

includes protons and neutrons (which together with electrons make up atoms) and K-mesons and a whole host of other exotic particles, such as pions, which whizz in from outer space. Once they had found this large number of new particles in the hadron family, scientists started trying to organize them into some sort of order. They found that if they made the assumption that all of the hadrons actually consisted of combinations of even smaller particles, they could explain the grouping of hadrons into branches of similar properties and masses. The most successful method of ordering these particles—called the 'Eightfold Way'—was invented in 1961 by Professor Gell-Mann, a physicist working in California. He proposed that all the particles revealed in the cloud chambers were combinations of what he called 'quarks[1].' He developed these ideas into a Standard Model of Particle Physics, which can now explain all of the observed particles in the universe as being combinations of two or three out of six elemental quarks. It was an astounding success for particle physicists and Gell-Mann was eventually awarded the Nobel Prize for this work. (Don't despair—I promise I'll be finished in a couple more pages.)

Gell-Mann and his colleagues called the six types of quark:

Introduction 前言

(last page) about $13.25 billion. These colliders smash together the nuclei of heavy elements, such as lead, at speeds only fractionally slower than that of light and then study the wreckage that flies off them.

1 He got this intriguing word from James Joyce, who wrote *Finnegan's Wake*, a book difficult even for quantum physicists. For some reason Joyce included the phrase, 'Three quarks for Muster Mark! Sure he hasn't got much of a bark, and sure any he has it's all beside the mark.'

Up | Down | Strangeness | Charm | Beauty | Truth[1]

Quarks cannot be observed individually because the attractive forces between them do not diminish as they become further apart.[2] When quarks are separated from one another, the energy in the surrounding field becomes so great that it immediately creates another quark-antiquark pair in space-time; quarks are thus forever bound up into their combinations and can only be seen amalgamated into observable hadrons. [3]

Quarks can only be inferred by watching the behaviour of their combinations; they cannot be observed alone. They are

---

1 When quark theory was first proposed, the two latest quarks were called 'beauty' and 'truth,' which was abbreviated 'B-quark' and 'T-quark.' Over time, the convention has changed so that it is now more common to call the B-quark 'Bottom' and the T-quark 'Top.' I have used the older convention.

2 This is called Colour Confinement. It means that quarks cannot be isolated singularly, and therefore (subject to note 3 below) cannot be directly observed. Quarks clump together to form hadrons. The two types of hadrons are called mesons (one quark, one antiquark) and baryons (three quarks) such as protons and neutrons. The constituent quarks in a group cannot be separated out of their parent hadron, and this is why quarks currently cannot be studied or observed in any more direct way than in combination as a hadron, a fact that cannot yet be explained by theory.

3 Free quarks probably did exist in the ultra-severe conditions in the few milliseconds after the Big Bang. Scientists at the Large Hadron Collider and the proton synchrotron at Brookhaven both think that they may have seen this phase of matter—called a quark-gluon plasma—after banging lead nuclei together at 99.99999% of the speed of light. It's amazing what people get up to these days. The collisions at Brookhaven took place at 4 trillion degrees centigrade and the Large Hadron Collider near Geneva reached 5.5 trillion.

sensed only when acting together and they are meaningful only within their larger context. In our world, the individual attributes of Up, Down, Strangeness, Charm, Beauty and Truth can never be seen directly. Quarks have been inextricably bound together by nature[1].

And here we get to the nub. Chinese poems, like quarks, and indeed like the radicals of Chinese characters, cannot be fully revealed in isolation; they cannot be understood on their own. They must be combined into a greater whole; they must be set into their own context and even then, they are wrapped up in uncertainty. The mathematicians may protest at this analogy; there is—obviously—no parallel between quantum chromodynamics[2] and Tang Dynasty poetry. Or is there?

Whenever I read about subatomic physics, I get a sense that the remarkable men and women—those marvellously devoted scientists slaving away in their particle colliders—they too have a sense of the mystic when they look inside subatomic particles. Who wouldn't, I suppose?

Perhaps we too should open our minds to this sense of wonderment that resides at the boundaries of human knowledge. The Nobel laureate Leon Lederman, for example, made a link

Introduction

前言

---

1   Or actually gluons but let's not go there.
2   Quantum chromodynamics is the name given to the mathematical description of quark interactions. It is very difficult to understand.

between God and the Higgs boson[1], infuriating some of his fellow physicists after it became known in the popular press as the 'God Particle.' But the physicists didn't need to choose the word 'charm' to describe one of the quarks or indeed the word 'strangeness.' And Professor Gell-Mann—when he initially proposed his quark model—he didn't need to choose the strangely haunting word 'quark,' nor did he need to call his theory the 'Eightfold Way' after the ancient Buddhist sutras.[2] And, Professor Hawking wasn't compelled to write that if he unified all four elemental forces in a 'Theory of Everything,' then we would 'know the mind of God.' But we should all be glad that they did choose these descriptors, because their choice of these particular and evocative words implies that the scientists, as well as the poets, are seeking their own 'God'—whatever or whomever that might be[3]—that they are seeking their own truth, elusive

---

1 The Higgs boson is an elementary particle in the Standard Model of Particle Physics and embodies the quantum excitation of the Higgs field. The presence of this field, now believed to be confirmed in the Large Hadron Collider, explains why some fundamental particles have mass when, based on symmetries controlling their interactions, they were expected to be massless.

2 The *Eightfold Way* is a guide written in the earliest times of history that sets out the Buddhist practices that can lead to liberation from the cycle of death and rebirth. The *Eightfold Way* teaches that by restraining oneself, cultivating discipline, and practicing mindfulness and meditation, one can attain nirvana and thus end the craving, clinging and karmic accumulations that cause all suffering.

3 Einstein, for example, seems to have believed in a pantheistic or all-encompassing 'God'—one where divinity exists within the whole

as it is, in each of their own different worlds. And their choice of language means that we can allow ourselves a sense of the miraculous even when—or perhaps especially when—we stop briefly on this journey towards the ancient Chinese poets to glimpse into the wondrous realm of subatomic particle physics.

(last page) of reality in a way that strangely resembles the Tao—and not an interventionist, personified God with will. He also called himself an agnostic rather than an atheist. Dirac, on the other hand, who predicted the existence of anti-matter by noting that the square root of a term in an equation defining mass can be both positive and negative, was an atheist who insisted that the criterion of mathematical truth is beauty. Personally, I find Clement Attlee's view on this topic most convincing. When asked if he was an agnostic, he replied 'I don't know!'

6

A General Theory of Chinese History

If Chinese poems and, indeed, the poets themselves, like quarks, can only be understood in overall combinations and once set into their wider context, what then is that context?

I ask for a moment to set the scene. Firstly, I will attempt to describe a narrative of China, with its over-arching themes and its dramas. Next I will move through the specific episodes unfolding whilst these poets lived and shamelessly borrow the nomenclature of Einstein's theories of relativity by forming a 'Frame of Reference' for our journey through this particular space and time. I will try to finish with a Special Theory of Chinese Poetry, and we'll see how it goes.

We set out by constructing a General Theory of Chinese History from three sets of observations.

Observation Number One: I should start at the very beginning, since it's a very good place to start. One can argue about the appropriate start point, but if we're searching for something near t=0 in Western civilisation, we could choose *Genesis* Chapter One? And if we so choose, the St James *Bible* version is probably as good as any:

'In the beginning God created the heaven and the earth. And the earth was without form, and void; and darkness was upon the face of the deep. And the Spirit of God moved upon the face of the waters. And God said, Let there be light: and there was light. And God saw the light, and it was good: and God divided the light from the darkness. And God called the light Day, and the darkness he called Night. And the evening and the morning were the first day.'

With these first words, we have immediately established a relationship between humankind and a personified, interventionist deity who—if we pursue the story much further—we find responds to prayer through a church that has, at times, claimed a monopoly on all instruments of communication. [1]

If, then, we were to turn our eyes eastwards and look for a similar moment at t=0 in the Chinese civilisation, what might we choose? Perhaps the opening words of the *Analects*? Let us listen to what Confucius has to say:

学而时习之，不亦说乎

有朋自远方来，不亦乐乎

人不知而不愠，不亦君子乎

---

1 Imagine what any sensible Anti-Trust legislation would make of that.

42

Is it not a pleasure to learn something new and put it into practice?

Is it not wonderful to have friends visit from afar?

When one's talents are not recognized, is it not better to rise above it all and remain unvexed?

These are surely thoughts that any human being in any society and at any time can identify with? Perhaps these two juxtaposed passages illustrate a basic difference between China and the West.[1] In the West, we seem to have developed certain axiomatic principles that flow from the relationship with God, principles that can't be debated but which need to be fought over whatever the precise circumstances, since they derive from the leap of faith required by religion. In China, the practical is much more to the fore. Whilst foreigners might spend hours wondering about other-worldly matters, debating principles, sometimes at the expense of results, and philosophising about the precise meaning of 'Is it a table?' the great minds of China were having their friends round for supper and getting plastered.[2] They seem

---

1 I should note in passing that there are of course many proverbs and parables in the *Bible* but not placed so centrally and at the beginning as with the *Analects*.

2 This must not be taken as trivialising Chinese thought, but rather emancipating the mind. After all, despite getting hammered with admirable regularity, the Chinese have built the longest lasting and arguably most successful state in history. And besides, some of the friends of Plato himself appeared quite sloshed at his *Symposium*.

to focus on the effect of actions rather than the principles that guide the original choice; the Chinese are much more concerned with results rather than the rules that must be followed in order to get there. Does Chinese thought follow the ideas of Jeremy Bentham more closely than those of Immanuel Kant?[1] Or to use the Chinese equivalent: 'What does it matter,' as they say, 'if a cat is black or white, so long as it catches mice.'

The first generalisation then is that the West lives more by the application of principles, whereas China looks largely to the 'result' and conforms to its own maxim— 'practice is the sole criterion of truth[2].'

Observation Number Two: my second point—and this isn't the result of any empirical research but just an accumulation of feelings whilst living in China for many years—is that history seems to play a much more significant role in the functioning of modern society in China than it does in the West. Chinese people seem to have a far stronger collective memory than we do and thus appear more connected to their past. [3] Living in China, one senses that history informs everything about the workings of the

Introduction

前
言

---

1 Or, as my son once asked in a pub, are they 'consequentialist rather than deontological?' whatever that means. He later explained—with what on the surface appeared to be the utmost patience but was subsequently revealed to be a delaying tactic applied ruthlessly to extract another round of beers from me—that deontological means 'guided by principle and less concerned with beneficial consequences.'

2 实践是检验真理的唯一标准

3 I admit this memory can at times be selective and depends on the ruler— the victor, after all, gets to write the history.

modern state in a way that has no parallel in the West; [1] and this characteristic may derive from the nature of the written word.

We have already seen that the Chinese language preserves a strong connection with the past because of the absence of verbal tenses; but the other important factor is the character-based nature of the language. The individual characters provide a link with the past quite unlike that provided by modern European languages. Characters represent complete ideas rather than just sounds so they are different to an alphabet in that they resist changes over the years or between regions. [2] Pronunciation of Chinese words might change over the centuries and across distance due to dialect, but the written character remains constant. The character 洟 may be pronounced '*ti*,' '*di*,' or '*tsi*' but it always means 'snivel.' [3]

---

1 I also admit that there is a contradiction here in that the Chinese have destroyed almost all of the physical manifestation of their ancient culture, whereas the Egyptians, for example, have preserved theirs to a remarkable degree. What I mean is that the Chinese consider their ancient thought to have direct operational relevance to solving a wide range of the problems of today whereas the Egyptians, Greeks and Italians do not invoke their ancient thought to tackle their current crises.

2 This was interrupted in the 1950's when hundreds of characters were simplified—such as 雲 changed to 云, and 靈 changed to 灵—in an effort to improve literacy. By doing that, a connection with the ancient origins of the language was partially broken.

3 This does not mean that the language is static. The meanings of some characters have evolved, whilst others have fallen out of use like, say, 'counterpane' or 'wainscot' in English, but ancient Chinese is much more understandable than our equivalent. One might even ask what written language we had in the eighth century at all? Whatever it was, it would not be comprehensible nowadays except to an expert.

Separate from the sound and recognizable over thousands of years, the characters keep history alive. When China's philosophers started to record their ideas on bamboo slips as far back as the sixth century BC, they used characters—such as 道 [1]—many of which are still in daily use. It's as if, with a little effort, the words of Plato or Aristotle leapt from the page in the original.

Until the last century this connection between the past and present was strengthened by a traditional dating system that provided no simple way to gauge relative historical periods. Dates were defined by the Emperor's reign; Jiaqing 18 was 1813 CE; Qiande 3 was 965 CE. There was nothing to indicate that one of the dates preceded the other by 848 years. The past seems to merge into the present in cycles that lack a clear timeline mapping stages in development or a precise origin where t=0.

In addition to casting history into quick-setting concrete, the character-based nature of the written word—in contrast to the phonetic—has two other consequences; firstly, the Chinese state was capable of administering the largest unified territory in the world because orders from the capital could be understood thousands of miles away even if the pronunciation was different; and, secondly, by combining art with meaning, the characters encouraged the development of a literati class of scholars that created a rich pool of educated talent capable of running the

Introduction 前言

---

1   'Road,' 'route' and, indeed, 'the Way' as in that of Laozi or Zhuangzi's
    teachings.

complex functions of a large and sophisticated state. These two factors—the reach of the characters across vast geographical distances and the development of a bureaucracy staffed with highly educated scholar officials[1]—facilitated economies of scale and the accrual of vast amounts of power in the hands of one man. Throughout history, during times of peace and stability, there have traditionally been limited competing power centres inside China apart from factions at the Court. There was no church[2], no parliament, no judiciary, no powerful land-owning aristocracy that could raise an army. Power on earth rested in the hands of 'The One Man'—the Emperor who perched, at times precariously, upon the Dragon Throne. History has bestowed the government in China with a unique role of wielding power unrestrained.

Having guessed at the reasons for its supremacy, we now need to consider what makes that government tick. The clues again come from history and the Chinese government is quite transparent in its primary motives; everything comes down to a

---

1　There may be another factor here in that the written language was complex so it prevented uneducated classes communicating and reaching any sort of critical mass that could challenge the State. It has been noted that throughout Chinese history, no new dynasty has been founded by a farmer who had read Sunzi's *Art of War*. Unsurprisingly, the insurrection was generally initiated by hungry and illiterate men who had absolutely nothing to lose.

2　The Buddhist 'church' did in fact become powerful enough in the CE 840's to attract a horrific purge by the Tang emperor, Wuzong, who issued an edict saying 'We will root out this pestilence...'

struggle for unity from the centre. For more than two thousand years, China has witnessed the rise and fall of successive dynasties with periods of stability followed by episodes of protracted chaos. In times of order, the economy prospered, the arts flourished; great cosmopolitan cities rose up on the back of commerce and trade; an ever more ingenious artisan class made pottery, iron, jade ornaments; great writers and philosophers shone new light on the world, painters mixed ever more brilliant pigments. Calligraphers made beautiful fox-hair brushes, [1] the granaries were full and the Chinese world enjoyed the blessings of peace. Then gradually power corrupted at the centre; taxes were diverted on their way to the capital and venal officials oppressed the peasantry without fear of punishment and sank into a life of indolence. Eventually, the dykes along the floodplains were no longer repaired, the granaries fell into ruin, the state failed to respond to natural disasters. Power ebbed from the capital and eventually it failed. The Empire sank into the abyss and endured perhaps a century of war, famine, disease, flooding and misery on a scale that is difficult to imagine. Finally, a peasant warlord would arrive with the militaristic instincts and utter ruthlessness necessary to bind the broken Kingdom together and the cycle started again.

Observation Number Three: a third idea is that the unification

---

1 The best brushes, as the more observant will notice later in the fourth line of the poem on page 111, were made from rabbit hairs.

of huge areas over prolonged periods of time facilitated the accumulation of a vast body of cultural and civilizational assets and material wealth, which attracted the envy of those on the outside. It is fairly obvious that at certain periods, say in the early eighth century, the Chinese really did have more going for them than anyone else at the time. As a result, the Chinese state, over the centuries, developed a fundamentally defensive rather than aggressive disposition. [1]

The Great Wall is, in many ways, the most powerful and ubiquitous symbol of China and is included as the central theme in the Chinese national anthem. If we try to think of a similarly potent emblem of the West, there is no real equivalent of a single physical structure, but the Cross might be a convincing candidate. Whilst the Cross is a symbol of different things to different people, an important aspect of Western religion has been the need to proselytize, the desire to go out and convert other societies to the Western point of view, whereas the Great Wall is exclusively and indisputably defensive. Kissinger described this difference by writing that the West claims moral exceptionalism, whereas the Chinese claim civilizational exceptionalism. There is a lot in that seemingly simple observation and it might explain why some Western countries embarked on military and colonial expeditions outside of their own territory, whereas the Chinese seemed more

---

1 However, there were subsequently costly wars aimed at recovering the territory within the Tang borders at their height.

content with what they'd already got.

The times that we will consider in the next section as we draw up our 'frame of reference' exhibit precisely the cycles of stability and chaos described above. After many centuries of turmoil, in 618, the Tang brought law and order to the suffering country. For the next century and a half, China enjoyed a 'Golden Age of Learning;' poets and painters excelled, strangers flocked to the capital and it became the largest and most cosmopolitan city in the world.[1] Traders from all four corners of the earth gathered there. The reign of the *Ming-huang*, or Brilliant Emperor from 712–756 was the culmination of the era. China's greatest poets were alive during his reign and the empire was at peace. However, the emperor gradually tired of the affairs of state; the court became indolent. He became obsessed with a beautiful consort called Yang and allowed one of her favourites—an obese general, possibly of Turkish descent, called An Lushan—to take command of three important garrisons in the north. In 755, An Lushan rebelled and captured Luoyang, the second city of China. After a power struggle at the Court and the appointment of an incompetent general, An's army broke through an important pass and marched on the capital. The Emperor panicked and fled towards the west. The following day, he was surrounded by his own soldiers demanding the

Introduction

前

言

---

1 Chang'an, which lay within the bounds of present day Xi'an in north-western China.

death of his consort Yang, whom they blamed for the disaster. Broken-hearted, he was forced to agree to her execution and she was strangled in the nearby temple by the Chief Eunuch. The emperor never recovered and pined for his lover for the rest of his life, thus providing a tale of endless sorrow that has inspired generations of poets ever since. [1]

After a series of protracted battles, the rebellion ended in 763, but the damage to the political economy from the rebellion was so great that the dynasty never really recovered. The census of 754 recorded fifty-three million people, but ten years later, another counted just seventeen, the shortfall presumably either in hiding, displaced or killed. Historians argue about the death-toll resulting from the An Lushan rebellion but in all probability, it was in excess of the First World War and represented a far greater proportion of the population. But whereas the toll in the First World War was inflicted with tanks and machine guns and poisonous gas, the carnage of the An Lushan rebellion was inflicted by spears and hatchets, hammer-maces, siege engines, catapults and bamboo cages filled with rocks and dropped down mountainsides on approaching armies.

These catastrophes happened at such regular intervals in China's long history that there's even—unusually—a specific

---

1   This series of events is captured in 'The Song of Unending Regret,' which starts on page 205, and which, whilst much shorter than, say, the *Iliad* or *Odyssey*, is nevertheless much longer than most Chinese poems.

word for the extreme and prolonged form of chaos, which does not have a parallel in our language; '*dà luàn*[1].' Successive dynasties rose and fell like a monstrous sine-wave traversing the centuries; we see the rise and fall of the Han, founded in 206 BC, then the short-lived Sui, and afterwards the Tang, Song, Yuan, Ming, and Qing, each lasting about three centuries and separated by a period of extreme suffering, until the last one finally collapsed in 1911. [2] In the last such cycle, China endured '*dà luàn*' chaos from the mid-1850's for almost a century until the last great peasant revolutionary united China and took his place in a long line of ancient philosopher kings stretching back to the time before Christ.

The Chinese government's basic task therefore is to maintain stability and to hold off another episode of '*dà luàn*' as far as possible. These cycles of stability and '*dà luàn*' explain why, in comparison to the West, social stability and collective responsibility in China are paramount. [3] This, then, is the context; let us now press onwards to the specific times of our chosen poets.

Introduction 前言

---

1   '*dà luàn*' is not mere anarchy, it is total war as if from the very depths of Rwanda or Aleppo but on a continent-wide scale. The Battle of Stalingrad or Hitler's siege of Leningrad might qualify, but only as a more geographically confined version that was also comparatively brief, lasting only a hellish 162 and 872 days respectively, rather than several decades.

2   The Yuan was rather shorter and only lasted a century.

3   I do not want to make any judgement about whether this is right or wrong but I think that it is important to explain and understand the reasons for it.

7
Frames of Reference

Within the overall narrative described above, the period that concerns us here is that of the Tang and Song Dynasties, a phase in Chinese history that spanned the six-and-a-half centuries from 618 CE to 1279 CE and gave rise to the greatest flowering of literature and art in the five-thousand year story of China. Has there ever been a time in history anywhere as creative, vigorous and productive? Whatever the more considered response to that question may be, we shall, in the meantime, use this period in Chinese history to build our own frame of reference for the onwards journey. We will find that, as the Tang and Song oscillated between order and chaos, the country endured decades of turmoil where people lived in fear of starvation or a violent and arbitrary death. But the thread that runs unbroken through these times, the thread that traverses the whole of Chinese history and binds it together so that it can survive the comprehensive collapse of its entire political economy, is the vast body of Chinese literature.

Tang

The Tang Dynasty was founded by Li Yuan, family patriarch and governor of the city of Taiyuan in northern China. He rose up in rebellion in 617 CE, supported by his daughter, who raised and commanded her own army with the utmost severity. Shortly after the governor declared himself the first emperor of the Tang on June 18 of that year, he was deposed by his son, Li Shimin[1], who had previously murdered both of his brothers. The son was to reign as the Taizong Emperor, the second of a long line that presided over a golden-age of peace and prosperity, culminating in the early part of the forty-four year reign of the *Ming-huang* Emperor in the following century.

53

---

1   I have been to the site of his mausoleum near Qian County in Shaanxi. It had been raining hard all morning and I was soaked, so I finally gave up on my bike and hailed a taxi. A narrow road wound up a mountain and into the clouds; damp mists swirled up the gullies around us. When we arrived at the tomb, the whole scene was shrouded in a dense, ghostly fog so I asked the driver to take me to the hotel; but he insisted I take a look. I found the deserted ticket gate and went inside, along a raised pathway through dark pines, past stone incense burners and over slippery steps up to a high terrace. Looming before me, wreathed in grey mist, was a huge statue of Li Shimin, flanked with three cloud columns on each side, seemingly leaning forwards and over me. I stood there for a long time, staring at this vast statue as it seemed to flicker and sway in the strange pale spectral light reflected from the rain-washed flagstones, whilst the wind soughed through the pine trees around me.

At its height, the Tang represented a pinnacle of the Chinese civilisation. Looking back through the rose-tinted mists of history, the Tang period appears as a well-ordered and harmonious society presided over by a benevolent, strict but loving emperor. I'm sure that the reality was more complicated. But the early Tang is now remembered as an era of peace and prosperity renowned for its leisure pursuits, such as feasting, drinking, tourism, hunting, archery, and even the odd tug-o'-war. Officials took holidays to visit their parents or organise their children's weddings. Spring Festival, the Lantern Festival and the Cold Food Festival were reserved as national holidays for everyone. Grand carnivals were held in celebration of military victories, good harvests and amnesties. One feast in 664 CE gathered together more than a thousand elders, another in 768 CE was attended by more than three thousand officers and, later on, the emperor held a banquet for twelve hundred women. Heavy drinking was almost considered a virtue.[1]

Chang'an, the Tang capital, was built on a chequer-board pattern, with the imperial palace on the central axis slightly towards the north. Elsewhere there were temples, shrines and abbeys with chanting monks and smoke rising from cast iron incense burners that drifted over the prayer halls. Buddhism had arrived in China and had been accepted as an official creed. [2]

---

1 But again, not the loutish version; it was meant to promote freedom of thought rather than action.

2 Though we must not forget the note on page 46.

In the government regulated markets, traders sold barley, soybeans, turnips, apricots, peaches, salt, garlic, chestnuts and walnuts. Restaurants served pork, chicken, lamb, sea otters, camels and even bears, though apparently they could be quite difficult to get hold of. Delicacies such as oysters (served with fine wine), horseshoe crabs and pufferfish, which the locals called 'river piglets,' were fished from the waters. The high-end taverns and whorehouses were staffed by courtesans trained with impeccable table manners and a perfect grasp of the complex rules of drinking games. Educated women of the time seem to have been treated with respect; records show that they were not afraid to castigate men who had spoiled dinner parties with their insufferably boring conversation, or even box the ears of those who tried to misbehave whilst drunk. Indeed, China at that time was ruled for a while by its only female monarch, the Empress Wu Zetian.

In this cosmopolitan atmosphere, the arts flourished. There was a highpoint in papermaking, sericulture, the high temperature glazing of celadon pottery, the art of seal carving, painting, calligraphy, mural decorations, ceramics, and carved laquer-ware; and the Tang produced some of the greatest poetry in the history of China.

However, in 755 CE, the dynasty was cut to pieces by the catastrophic uprising of An Lushan. As described earlier, although the regime survived, it was so weakened that it relinquished control over agriculture and commerce. By 845 CE, there were reports of bandits and river pirates plundering settlements along the Yangtse without resistance from the army. Massive flooding along the Grand Canal in 858 CE convinced many that the dynasty had lost its Mandate of Heaven.[1] A horrific famine rocked the empire to its foundations in 873 CE when it proved incapable of responding to the crisis. There was then a period of widespread insurrection and turmoil before the dynasty finally collapsed in 907 CE. In conformity with that dreadful and inevitable cycle, China sank into five decades of turmoil and disaster known as the Five Dynasties and Ten Kingdoms before it was again reunited under the Song. That dynasty was to last for the following three centuries from 960 CE until 1279 CE.

---

1   The Mandate of Heaven is a principle used to justify the power of the emperor, but it comes at a cost. According to this belief, heaven bestows its mandate only to a just ruler, who must earn it through the virtuous administration of the empire; if he does not fulfill his obligations as an ethical and competent ruler, then he loses the Mandate and thus the right to be emperor. It was common belief that heaven sent natural disasters such as famine and flood as signs of a dynasty nearing its end, thus there were often revolts following major environmental events since they were interpreted as celestial displeasure. For example, after a colossal unexplained explosion in Wanggongchang in south-western Beijing on the morning of 30th May, 1626, which killed 20,000, obliterated much of Beijing and hurled debris for 30 kilometers but left almost no fire damage locally, the Tianqi Emperor was widely criticized for offending Heaven through his obsession with carpentry and his almost total neglect of his duties.

Song

The Song empire—like the Tang—can be divided into two phases, but in this case it was separated by an invasion rather than an internal rebellion. The invasion forced a permanent move of the capital from the city of Kaifeng in the north to Hangzhou, the great cultural centre that lies around a lake towards the south, nearby to present-day Shanghai. Thus the Song is divided into two periods; the Northern Song from 960 CE to 1127 CE and the Southern Song from 1127 CE to 1279 CE. Throughout the Song period, the population doubled from about a hundred million to two. Our poets either lived in the earlier phase of the Northern Song or spanned the rebellion.

After the first Song emperor, Taizu, brought the country together again, he focused on binding it ever more tightly by reforming the imperial exam system[1], improving the postal systems and compiling a compendium of maps that covered all the major administrative centres.

Social life in Song Dynasty China was on a par with the Tang at its height. Connoisseurs traded fine artworks; the spread of literature was encouraged by the invention of first woodblock printing and then of moveable type. To keep up with the times,

Introduction　前言

1　The fall of the Tang had scattered and destroyed the aristocracy that had staffed the imperial bureaucracy.

philosophers such as Zhu Xi reinvigorated Confucianism by adding commentary and reorganising the main texts. At its peak, the Song was by far the largest and wealthiest state on the planet. Rice cultivation was expanded by the introduction of early ripening strains from Central Asia, which enabled the state to produce and store surpluses in a system of imperial granaries. The Song introduced retirement homes, public clinics and paupers' graveyards. Women enjoyed certain property rights and, whilst it was hardly a panacea of gender equality, many were noted for their high education and literary achievements. In the cities, puppeteers and snake charmers mixed with acrobats, sword-swallowers and the medieval equivalent of rappers who recited poetry to the rhythmic beating of wooden clappers[1]; there were teahouses and theatres which could seat thousands.

A famous scroll painted in the early twelfth century depicts one day in the life of the Song capital. Known as *Qing Ming Festival on the River*, it moves across both space and time—like the tracks in the cloud chambers—and starts at the extreme right end of the scroll at dawn with fishing boats being launched quietly into the river. As the eye moves towards the left, we follow the progress of the day along the banks of the river. By lunchtime, we reach a crowded bridge, placed perfectly in the middle of the

---

1 I once saw the modern equivalent in Xi'an in 1988, and it is still performed in rural villages in Shaanxi today.

scroll, festooned with flags and surrounded by busy restaurants serving steamers full of dumplings. Later in the day and further towards the left, the teahouses are filled with customers before we complete the day at the end of the scroll with a camel train tramping out of the city under a magnificent gateway at the start of a long journey. [1]

Throughout the provinces, the law was enforced by travelling sheriffs and well-trained court judges who meted out punishments, including severe foot-whipping and striking of

---

1 The scroll is ten inches high and just under six yards long. It includes eight hundred people, twenty-eight boats, sixty animals, thirty buildings and many trees and sedan chairs. The river meanders through the whole picture. In the fields outside the city, there are unhurried rural folk—peasant farmers, goatherds, pig tenders. Country paths converge on a road that leads towards the city. Further in, labourers load cargo into boats, shop counters heave with goods for sale and there is even a tax office. There are peddlers, jugglers, actors, beggars, monks, fortune tellers, doctors, innkeepers and carpenters. On the bridge, there is a great commotion as a large vessel appears to be approaching out of control, with its mast still raised. The crowds on the bridge shout and gesticulate at the boat as someone lowers a rope to the crew below. It is probably the most famous painting in China and has been described as China's *Mona Lisa*, although the subject and techniques are totally different. The scroll can hold attention for a long while because of the vivid action, the movement in the picture and the astounding details that reveal ordinary lives within the sophisticated world that existed so far back in time. I once flew from Beijing to Hong Kong to go to a rare exhibition of the scroll—it is only shown every five years or so. I pitched up at the gallery only to find that it was completely sold-out for the coming six weeks. Hong Kong has a population of six million and many of those queuing were in their teens.

Introduction 前言

the buttocks with bamboo clappers. New techniques in forensic science were used in criminal cases to determine whether murder victims showed signs of strangulation, drowning, beating or poisoning.

Poems became the dominant mode of expression in both high literature and folklore and were assembled into huge encyclopaedic collections, such as *The Poems of a Thousand Masters*, together with historiographies and political treatise, such as the monster *Comprehensive Mirror for Aid of Governance*[1], which was published in 1084 CE and summarised the history of the previous eleven dynasties. It consists of 294 volumes, which—eight centuries later—Mao read again and again, stacked up around his huge bed, searching ceaselessly for meaning right up until the end of his life.[2]

By the middle of the eleventh century, the burst of economic and social activity under the Song caused severe stresses within the Chinese political class. The inevitable cycle of stability and chaos slowly turned. Growing complexities in society provoked

---

1 《资治通鉴》

2 At the same time as it was written, there were huge strides in technology, mathematics, philosophy, the sciences and engineering which were summarised in the great collection of innovations, the *Tian Gong Kai Wu* or *The Exploitation of the Works of Nature*. Although it was published much later at the end of the Ming period, many of the inventions came from the Song. The encyclopaedia covers a wide range of skills, from irrigation to sericulture, the extraction of mercury, salt technology, metallurgy, papermaking and, of course, fermented beverages.

intense arguments about policy at court. Attempts to modernise the bureaucracy and establish a government monopoly on salt to raise indirect taxation and redistribute wealth caused an intense backlash from the conservative factions. [1] Embittered and protracted power struggles distracted and weakened the Court until, on 9 January 1127 CE, a huge rebel army poured in from the north and ransacked the Song capital. That army was commanded by the *Jin*, who were descended from the Jurchen tribe and originally inhabited the forests and rivers to the extreme north-east. Driving southwards through China, they captured both the Song Emperor Qinzong and his father, Emperor Huizong, who had abdicated in panic in the face of the invasion. The court was forced to flee to the southern city of Hangzhou and the Southern Song continued to wage war against the *Jin* for a further decade before they eventually signed a peace treaty in 1141 CE. The shift of capitals from Kaifeng to Hangzhou was the dividing line between the Northern and Southern Song dynasties.

Although the Song Dynasty had lost control of the Yellow

61

Introduction 前言

---

1 Karl Marx would have approved as he sat in the British Library eight centuries later. It has been reported widely in foreign literature that the famous Song Chancellor Wang Anshi wrote: 'The State should take the entire management of commerce, industry and agriculture into its own hands with a view to succouring the working classes and preventing them from being ground into the dust by the rich. ' Sadly I can find no record of this idealistic sentiment in the original Chinese.

River basin—the birthplace of the Chinese civilization—its economy remained strong. It still controlled a large population and most of China's productive agricultural land. It used this wealth to build ships for both domestic and maritime trade and constructed huge harbours with beacons and warehouses. At a battle on the Yangtse in 1161 CE, the Song used fast paddle boats for the first time armed with huge counterweight catapults, which launched powerful gunpowder bombs at their enemies. Soldiers were armed with 'fire lances' which discharged flames and shrapnel. Military capacity increased and the arsenals were stocked with explosive grenades, cannons and landmines.

At the same time the Song strengthened the recruitment of competent officials by reforming and enhancing the system of imperial exams. These measures helped shift China from a society that was dominated by the military and powerful family elites towards one that was governed by more competent and well-educated literati, or 'scholar-officials,' selected on merit. Joint stock companies were formed, huge vessels transported goods up the Yangtse and through the Grand Canal. The iron industry had smelters that produced millions of tons each year, which would have consumed entire forests had not coal been substituted for charcoal.

Yuan

Peace reigned until the empire was once again assailed from

the north by Mongol armies driven across the frozen steppes by Genghis Khan. In 1271 CE, the Song eventually succumbed to his grandson, Kublai Khan, who became the first emperor of the Yuan Dynasty and set his capital close to the boundaries of modern day Beijing. But the wheel of history still turned; whilst Kublai Khan had been cruel and efficient during his early years as emperor, the familiar corruption and indolence soon set in. He became grotesquely fat, suffering dreadfully from gout, and held endless banquets of meat and *koumiss*, a type of alcoholic fermented mare's milk. Abandoning government, just like the *Ming-huang* Emperor of the Tang, he was in a near continual state of inebriation. At his hunting reserve, four elephants would carry him, lying on a couch, in a gold plated palanquin decked with tigerskins, accompanied by five hundred falconers and leopards and lynxes trained to chase down bears and wild boars. His dynasty suffered the inevitable fate and collapsed in 1368 CE.

Introduction 前言

8
A Special Theory of Chinese Poems

Now on to the heart of the matter—what does all of this mean? Why should anyone care?

According to legend, the earliest Chinese poems might date from as early as the twenty-third century BCE and consist of short, pithy songs, such as the 'Earth Drumming Song,' which may have been chanted by farmers as they worked on the land:

日出而作	When the sun comes out, we work,
日入而息	When it goes in, we rest.
凿井而饮	When we dig wells, we drink,
耕田而食	When we plough fields, we eat.
帝力于我何有哉	Huh! What is the Emperor's power to us?

Almost two millennia later, by the time of Confucius (551–479 BCE), a written tradition had developed and the Great Sage himself is said to have complied a collection of 305 poems in the *Book of Songs*, which consisted of unattributed rhythmic ballads, folk stories and chants. Five hundred years later, around the time of Christ, a further collection was published, called the *Book of Chu*, that contained the work of known poets expressing the joys and sorrows of human existence in a more personal and heartfelt manner. A further millennium passed before a collection of comparable importance emerged at the end of the Song, *The Poems of the Thousand Masters*. It was complied by Liu Kezhuang (1187–1269 CE) and was arranged in categories. Liu chose the fourteen topics of flowers, bamboo, the heavens, the earth, palace life, weather, tools, music, animals, insects, seasons, festivals, daily events and human character. As his book closely followed the invention of printing, its influence was widespread, especially on the education system. These three standard texts represent the distillation of tens of thousands—possibly hundreds of thousands—of poems that survive across the centuries and inform every aspect of Chinese thought. Rote learning of the classics from the *Thousand Masters* has been a requirement at school since that time right up to the present day, with only a brief interlude during the Cultural Revolution (1966–1976 CE). School students in China today still have to learn by heart a large body of poetry and annotations. At the time they generally hate it, but later in life they often derive great pleasure from reciting the poems learned at school from memory.

Through this long process, poetry has come to define the

Chinese civilisation like no other art form. China's greatness in painting, high-glazed ceramics, architecture, theatre and dance, the casting of bronzes, the early sculpting of terracotta is all revered throughout the world, but poetry is China's defining art form and universally appreciated and participated in throughout society and history.

The character for 'poem'—诗 or 'shī'— is composed of two parts: 讠, the radical meaning 'language,' and the phonetic 寺, meaning 'court' or 'temple.' I have read[1] that the character was originally written 誌, consisting of 言 and 志, and pronounced 'zhì,' and that the modern day version arose from some sort of calligraphic shorthand. This character 志 is again composed of two parts: 士, meaning 'scholar,' and 心, meaning 'heart.' Hence the word for poem originally amalgamated the concept of 'scholarship' and 'language,' with that of 'the heart.' The preface to the *Book of Songs* tried to describe poetry as follows:

在心为志   When in the heart, it's *zhì*,

发言为诗   when expressed in language, it's *shī*.

Thus, since the dawn of civilisation 5,000 years ago, it has

---

1   There is an excellent translation of the *Thousand Masters* called *Poems of the Masters* by Red Pine, which is the pen name of the American scholar Bill Porter. I gratefully acknowledge my debt to his analysis of Chinese poetry which has inspired many of the ideas in this section.

been the function of poetry to express the innermost feelings and beliefs, and the deepest, most secret hopes of the beating Chinese heart. It is the ultimate distillation of the meaning and beauty that can be found in the Chinese characters. The unchanging nature of the character-based language provides a coherence and continuity to Chinese poetry that has no parallel in other civilisations. Yet, at the very kernel of the poem lies a void that arises out of ambiguity, a void that allows the reader space to interpret the sentiments in a way that fits their own experience. This central paradox, the emptiness, the non-existence at the heart of these poems, which have nevertheless been constructed so meticulously according to rigid millennia-old rules, create for the reader an experience almost like meditation, where one meets an undifferentiated emptiness, where self and the world's constructs dissolve away.

Poetry encapsulates the essence of traditional Chinese culture and belief; the ease with nature; the view that man is but one part of a wider universe; that all attempts to dominate non-human nature are futile. It speaks of the shifting balances between natural forces, such that the anthropogenic aspects of climate change are more readily accepted in Chinese society as self-evident. [1] The verses show a sense of outrage at injustices and,

Introduction 前言

---

1 'How can you not expect nature to react against you if you spend two centuries digging trillions of tons of coal out of the ground and burning it into the sky?' they ask.

at the same time, the dangers attendant on protest. Some poems were used as political weapons, right from the first unifying Qin emperor who burned the books, through to Mao two millennia later, who seemed at times like a philosopher-king, moving on a different and higher plane, achieving a kind of weaponisation of odes. Elsewhere, in happier lines, there is a soft, self-mocking humour that illustrates the effects of passing time on mind and body. We find a yearning to shake off the shackles of convention and breathe the fresh air. We follow the search for peace in the solitude of a hermit, which—as sulking taken to the ultimate degree—was also considered an act of protest through the deliberate absenting of oneself from society and government service.

At the height of the Tang and Song, nothing was significant without a poem; no social occasion or ritual, no personal event or gathering was complete without at least a few lines to capture that fleeting moment. Poetry was everywhere. It still is—on walls outside factories, in the street, in households, in inns and restaurants, monasteries, on hoardings in town squares. It is used copiously in speeches by politicians or in conversation between friends or colleagues to illustrate or drive home a point. It entertains; it insults. It persuades, it paints pictures in the air, it enflames loyalty, it soothes the ire of a rebellious youth. Thus, we can use these poems as a window into this inner world of Chinese thought and imagination. Such is the reverence still accorded to poetry amongst Chinese people that any passing knowledge of it, even in your own language passing through a translator, will inspire friendships in China; it will add weight and meaning to your interactions with people there; it will explain better what it is that you find around you; it will enlarge your capacity for understanding and empathy. It will present you as someone interested in the experience of life itself and demonstrate an appreciation of all that is universal, all that is human. It will, in the words of Samuel Johnson, give you the 'lustre' of someone who 'had gone to view the wall of China.' [1] It expresses feelings that transcend culture and are common to all civilisations and therefore it has direct operational relevance to everyday life in China because it allows you to communicate on a deeper level. You will be more effective in whatever it is you want to achieve in China and people there will like you.

---

1 The full quote is recounted to us in *The Life of Samuel Johnson* by James Boswell, 1791, as follows: "He talked with an uncommon animation of travelling into distant countries, that the mind was enlarged by it and that an acquisition of dignity of character was derived from it. He expressed a particular enthusiasm with respect to visiting the wall of China. I catched it for the moment (sic) and said I really believed I should go and see the wall of China had I not children of whom it was my duty to take care. 'Sir,' said he, 'by doing so you would do what would be of importance in raising your children to eminence. There would be a lustre reflected upon them from your spirit and curiosity. They would be at all times regarded as the children of a man who had gone to view the wall of China. I am serious, sir!' "

9

The Second Thread to Bind an Empire

As society swung between order and chaos, poetry provided a continuity that survived the ages. Whilst literature bound together the social fabric of imperial China, a second thread bound together the Chinese state—the system of imperial '*ke-ju*' examinations. The mutually reinforcing interplay between them to a large degree accounts for the robustness of the Chinese civilisation.

As we have seen, poetry was wide ranging and spanned the celebration of nature or friendship, the venting of grief, political infighting, the advancement of courtship. It was composed by emperors, warlords and commanders, monks, courtesans, city dwellers and amongst farm folk, but above all, by the scholar officials who emerged from the *ke-ju* examinations. Thus the *ke-ju* had both a profound influence on the development of poetry but at the same time, the *ke-ju* in later times reflected the achievements of the earlier masters.

For much of the time since the Han—who came to power in 206 BCE—through to the last century and arguably up to the present day, the people who ran China have been selected by exams.

Before the *ke-ju*, officials were selected according to recommendation or family connections, but Han Wudi—the great unifying Han emperor who ruled from 141–87 BCE—initiated a rudimentary precursor of the exam system by using competitions that tested skill. The formal *ke-ju* system was instated in the short-lived Sui Dynasty in 605 CE. It was progressively strengthened, systematised and improved under the Tang, with the introduction of questions on policy as well as oral examinations on poetry and other topics. In 681 CE, a test was introduced requiring the memorisation of large blocks of the classics. Twelve years later, the intake was widened to include people who were not part of an elite family because the ruler, Wu Zetian—China's only Empress—needed officials loyal to her to run the bureaucracy. The subsequent collapse of the Tang destroyed the powerful elite of families and cemented the *ke-ju* system as a central plank of Chinese society.

As it developed into a written form, the exam system had the effect of unifying culture; the State decided which of the classical texts should be emphasised and which should be forgotten. In the following Song Dynasty, candidacy for the exam widened across society and many people of lowly birth were able to achieve high rank and prominence through success at the exams. Most people were eligible to try the exams, but from time to time there were

Introduction 前言

peculiar restrictions on various groups, such as sorcerers, beggars, boat people, sex workers and butchers.

The final exams used to take place over three days and two nights in the capital. Candidates were locked into isolated cells containing nothing but two wooden boards that could be arranged as a bed or at different levels as a desk and bench. Candidates were allowed to take in a pitcher of water, a chamber pot, bedding, an ink-stone, ink and brushes and they were held completely *incommunicado* for the full three days. If a student died, he was wrapped in straw and thrown over the high walls of the examination compound. Incessant and ever more ingenious methods of cheating were devised by the candidates. Vast tracts of classical literature were diligently sewn into underpants by anxious grandmothers or hidden in food or body cavities. In 992 CE, as part of an attempt to stamp out endemic bribery, the mandarins required the papers to be submitted anonymously. But the bribery persisted until, in 1105 CE, the emperor insisted that the answers should be copied and rewritten so that handwriting could not be recognised by examiners.

Whilst this system promoted cohesion across vast distances, its insistence on the regurgitation of rote-learned classics within the traditional structure of an 'eight-legged' essay naturally throttled creativity. It moulded ideas into ancient casts and, by creating uniformity of thought, it achieved the state's aim of avoiding *dà luàn* chaos by promoting social order.

Even those who failed the exams were not discarded. Imbued in the traditional thought of ancient China, those who could not reach the top grades were employed to oversee detailed day-to-day work rather than grand strategy. They took on the maintenance of the irrigation systems, dykes and the imperial granaries and worked as teachers, tax inspectors and as patrons of art.

The *ke-ju* was abolished only in 1905. The current system used by the Chinese Communist Party to select the most capable officials at the Cadre Training School by the Summer Palace in Beijing has been influenced by this ancient system because the aim is still to select the best possible leadership with a unified group with similar views and alignments. Thus the exams are possibly the longest lasting institution in any civilisation in history and was a key resource in the successful governance of what was at most times in the past millennia, the largest, most successful and sophisticated state on the planet. It existed in juxtaposition to the achievements of the poets, both informing them of the classical themes and locking them into a rigid pattern of expression, but at the same time, adapting to include the art of the later periods as they became part of the overall Chinese scene.

Introduction 前言

10
Who, Then, Were These Masters?

The seventy poems collected here were written mainly during the Tang and the Song periods. I have concentrated on seven poets—six men and one woman[1]—although others are included as well.

As we have seen, poetry in China dates from very early times. Much later, the First Masters wrote during the fourth and fifth centuries, so the Tang poets, who followed a couple of centuries

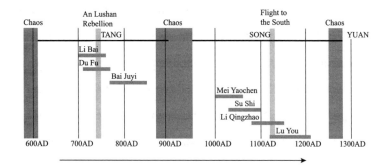

Timeline of the Seven Tang and Song Poets

1　Rest assured this is no tokenism. Female poets were not unusual in imperial China, but the work of many was later destroyed by envious men, who knew they weren't as good. Part of Li Qingzhao's work survived and it is right up there with the best of them.

later, represent a renaissance rather than fundamentally new ideas.

A timeline showing the period in which the seven poets wrote is shown in the chart above. As always in China, it includes periods of prosperity and peace broken apart by episodes of severe social turmoil, indicated in shade.

Li Bai

The first to walk onto our stage is Li Bai (701–762 CE) also known as the *Zhexianren*, or 'Banished Immortal.' His life was characterized by wistful travel through fantastic natural landscapes, by wild drinking parties, where friends would leap up in a sudden frenzy, grab a brush and create vast panoramas of almost unintelligible characters—and by a deliberate disdain for accepted manners and authority. His poems have the feel of a detached spirit roaming the world with an unearthly freedom, treading a pathway through the wild and natural world rather than being locked into the concerns of society. One can feel that Li Bai benefited from living most of his creative life in a time of stability and peace.

Introduction 前言

Li Bai is generally believed to have been born in what is now Kyrgyzstan, where his family had built up a successful trading business. The family moved back to a village in the south-western province of Sichuan when he was around five years old.

76

In that rural setting, he became skilled in taming wild birds, in swordsmanship, riding and hunting, and before he was twenty, he had fought and killed several men. In 720 CE, he was interviewed by the Provincial Governor, who concluded that he was a genius. Possibly for personal reasons, Li Bai never sat the imperial examinations. Instead, he embarked on a prolonged period of wandering, traversing vast distances over many years, including long voyages along China's major rivers. By 740 CE, he seems to have settled for a while in Shandong, where he joined a group called 'The Six Idlers of Bamboo Brook,' an informal gathering dedicated to an appreciation of literature and the simultaneous consumption of truly catastrophic quantities of alcohol.

In 742 CE, Li Bai was summoned to court by the *Minghuang* Emperor, where his writing and personality proved fascinating to the court, particularly as he was often summoned to an audience in a state of profound drunkeness, yet still managed to perform perfectly. Li Bai met fellow poet Du Fu in the autumn of 744 CE when they shared a room and enjoyed common interests, such as hunting, travel, wine and poetry, thus becoming close and lasting friends. In 755 CE, the state fell into disorder during the An Lushan rebellion. Li Bai was caught up in court intrigue and sentenced to death but before the sentence could be carried out, a sympathetic General swapped his title in return for Li Bai's life and the punishment was commuted to banishment to the remote and desolate province of Gansu.

Despite this sentence, Li Bai headed off with little sign of hurry, and stopped off for social visits on the way, some of which lasted months and entailed feasting, drinking and writing. Li Bai never made it to Gansu and continued his wanderings until he died in Anhui.[1] There is a story that he drowned, blind drunk, after falling out of his boat during a conversation with the reflection of the moon. Even if the story is not true, Li Bai is likely to have died from the effects of his hard-living lifestyle. A famous American translator of Li Bai's poems wrote:

'nearly all Chinese poets celebrated the joys of wine, but none so tirelessly and with such a note of genuine conviction as Li Bai.'

Du Fu

Next comes Du Fu (712–770 CE) also known as the *Shisheng*, or 'Poet Sage.' Du Fu is considered by many as the greatest in China's history and more than 1,500 of his poems survive. Many of the later poems touch on the great themes of history and the moral dilemmas that events force upon us. Du Fu was also inspired by his closeness to nature and the pleasures of friendship.

Du Fu's writing was greatly influenced by social turmoil; he

Introduction　前言

1　Li Bai was on these travels and in exile in the south when Du Fu wrote the poem 'Dreaming of Li Bai' in 759 CE on page 223.

was forty-four[1] when the An Lushan rebellion convulsed China. After rebel armies overran the capital, Du Fu was captured but he escaped and hid in a monastery, an experience which left him deeply shaken. The dire social situation is a constant theme in Du Fu's later poems and he was the first poet to write about real, immediate social concerns.

Despite having failed the *ke-ju* exams—a fact that has puzzled historians ever since—Du Fu spent several years trying to help the government re-establish order, but failed completely. For the rest of his life, he never really settled, nor did he stop agonizing about the country's struggles. Du Fu's poetry is infused with a restless wandering; he gives us an exile's view on the vast human drama and suffering caused by war. He stands poised between black despair and an exquisitely sensibility towards the agonies and hopes of the refugee fleeing the warzone.

Du Fu was born somewhere near Luoyang in northern China and his mother died shortly afterwards. He had several half-siblings to whom he refers frequently in his poems, but he never mentions his step-mother. As mentioned earlier, in 735 CE, he took the civil services exams and failed, a fact that has mystified scholars ever since. It may have been that his style was too advanced for the examiners to understand fully. When

---

1   According to Chinese year counting.

he met Li Bai in 744 CE, the older poet had a great influence on Du Fu partly because of the age difference but also because Li Bai lived in a manner that was close to the classical ideal of the reclusive poet-scholar. Two years later Du Fu moved to the capital to try to resurrect his career as an official and took the exams again in 747 CE, but this time the whole cohort was failed by the Prime Minister, who was obsessed with preventing rivals progressing up the imperial bureaucracy.

Du Fu married shortly afterwards and had five children. As explained above, in 755 CE, his life changed forever after the outbreak of the An Lushun rebellion, which caused a complete breakdown in civil society. After his capture, he was taken back to Chang'an, which had fallen to rebels. Separated from his family, he may also have contracted malaria at this time. Du Fu's life was spared because he was of too lowly rank to be important. Once reunited with his family, Du Fu was forced to move again by a famine brought on by massive flooding. Despite his suffering—Du Fu's youngest child died around this time—Du Fu was not self-pitying and referred sympathetically to the predicament of others caught in the turmoil around him:

> *'Brooding on what I have lived through,*
> *if even I know such suffering,*
> *the common man must surely be rattled by the winds.'*

Shortly afterwards, he was sent to Huazhou[1] as a minor official. It was not to his liking:

> *'I am about to scream madly in the office,*
> *especially when they bring more papers*
> *to pile yet higher on my desk.'*

In 759 CE, Du Fu travelled to Chengdu in Sichuan, where he spent five years in the warm climate and away from the war. Despite financial problems, it seems to have been a happy and productive time in his life and many of his poems from that period show him at peace, living in his 'thatched hut.' After his birthplace, Luoyang, was recovered by the Emperor in the winter of 762 CE, Du Fu set sail down the Yangtse to return to his roots. The party travelled slowly, held up by his health, and stopped off at a place called Baidicheng for two years, where he wrote 400 poems in his characteristic dense style. They set off again for Luoyang, but Du Fu died on the journey in Hunan at the age of 58.

Bai Juyi

The second phase of the Tang, after the rebellion, enjoyed

---

1   It was during his time in Huazhou, Shaanxi, that Du Fu came across the Pressgang in Stone Moat Village, which he recorded in his poem on page 137.

a degree of stability but society was nevertheless always haunted by war. The main character in this period was Bai Juyi (772-846 CE) who was born into a lower level but well-educated family living on the edge of poverty. He passed the imperial exams and, by the age of thirty-six, he was an advisor to the Emperor. Though he was well known by his middle age, Bai never forgot his earlier impoverished existence. He was always outspoken in his support for ordinary people struggling in penury and burdened with taxes, and was highly critical of inept officials and chronic militarism.[1] As Bai's poetry became more popular, it stirred up passions for better social justice amongst ordinary people and thus attracted the ire of conservative factions at the court. Bai was exiled and abandoned this style of poetry, continuing as a minor official until he retired to a renovated monastery in northern China in 832 CE, where he spent his later years organising and codifying his life's work.

Also known as *Letian*, meaning 'happy-go-lucky,' Bai Juyi was born in the north-west and was a devout Buddhist throughout

---

1 As I read some of Bai Juyi's lines on this 'chronic militarism,' I could not help but think of Eisenhower's farewell speech as president more than a millennium later, as he left the White House and warned about the 'immense military establishment and large arms industry' in the US and its 'total influence—economic, political, even spiritual —felt in every city, every Statehouse, every office of the Federal government. We must' he went on, 'guard against (the vast military-industrial complex's) acquisition of unwarranted influence, whether sought or unsought. The potential for the disastrous rise of misplaced power exists and will persist.'

his life.

———————————

Bai moved south to Henan in early childhood. His father was an Assistant Magistrate of the Second Class, so the family was poor but scholarly. In 800 CE, he passed the *ke-ju* examinations. Shortly afterwards, his career was interrupted when his father died and Bai had to take the obligatory period of two years mourning, retiring to the banks of the Wei River. As soon as he returned, with the utmost inconvenience, his mother promptly died so he had another several years of mourning on top of the last. When he finally returned to Court, he fell out of favour after writing several poems mocking the greed of senior officials and contrasting it with the suffering of ordinary people. His enemies used his poems to accuse him of impiety, which was a grave offense in the Confucian world; his mother had died after falling into a well whilst looking at some flowers, and Bai had written several poems, one of which was entitled 'In Praise of Flowers.' As a result, he was banished from the Court and sent to a remote place in Sichuan as a governor.[1] In 819 CE, he was recalled to the capital, but found that the new emperor spent most of his time feasting and drinking whilst the empire crumbled. He was again banished after writing critical memorials and sent to Hangzhou as governor, where he greatly improved the lives of ordinary people

———————————

1   It was in Sichuan that Bai planted up a garden, as described in the poem on page 243.

by repairing the dykes around West Lake. In 825 CE, at the age of fifty-three, Bai was given the governorship of Suzhou but became ill shortly afterwards. He spent the rest of his life, nominally in posts around Luoyang, but in reality in retirement organising his Collected Works and he died there in 846 CE, leaving instructions for a simple burial. His circular burial mound still sits on the banks of the Yi River with the simple inscription, 'Bai Juyi.'

Bai Juyi was not without critics during his lifetime. One, a fellow poet, wrote:

'It has bothered me that ... we have had poems by Bai Juyi... whose sensual poetry has defied the norms. Apart from gentlemen of mature strength and classical decorum, many have been ruined by them. They have circulated among the common people and been inscribed on walls; mothers and fathers teach them to sons and daughters orally. Through winter's cold and summer's heat, their scandalous phrases and overly familiar words have entered people's flesh and bone and cannot be washed out. I have no position and cannot use the law to bring this under control.'

That's an epitaph to strive for.

Mei Yaochen

Our first Song era poet is Mei Yaochen (1002−1060 CE).

Allegedly a tall, well-natured man, with bushy eyebrows and large ears, Mei is remembered for his deliberately artless simplicity, his self-styled *pingdan* style, which means 'bland,' 'thinned-out' or 'flavourless' and is meant to emphasise the search for naturalness and understatement in writing rather than ostentatious ornamentation. He took experience 'as-it-is' rather than trying to extract emotional or philosophical meaning from it. He eschewed the flourishes and exaggeration of 'art-for-art's-sake' and intentionally wrote about subjects that were traditionally regarded as unworthy of poetry such as the experience of caring for small children. Through this, he challenged the idea that some thoughts were lofty whilst other were prosaic and thus put himself beyond choosing what was and what was not valuable.

Mei Yaochen was born in central Anhui Province to a poor peasant family. When he was sixteen, he went with his uncle to the major northern city of Luoyang as his family could no longer support his education. It was in Luoyang that Mei was to meet fellow poets and join a new poetic movement which held that literature should mirror ordinary life, rather than consist of the then-fashionable romantic overblown ballads which were full of flourishes and hyperbole. Thus many of Mei's poems describe ordinary everyday events in what he called 'an easy-going voice.'

Whilst serving in several minor posts as an official in Jiande County in Anhui, Mei gained a reputation as a sympathetic man who would talk to 'brick-bakers and poor women' to understand the cares and sorrows of their troubled lives. Records show that he personally supervised flood relief works and the efforts to control wildfires on the local mountain slopes. He also won the affections of local people for replacing the dilapidated bamboo enclosure around the township with earth walls after previous officials had made excuses for not doing so—and probably embezzled the money, who knows? After he left the post, the citizens expressed their gratitude by changing the name of the township to Mei City, a name that still persists today. Mei Yaochen finally passed the top level of the imperial exams in 1051 CE under the Emperor Renzong when he was 49. He left over three thousand poems in a marvelously quirky voice, which he modestly characterized as 'ordinary and tranquil.'

Su Shi

Next comes the great intellectual Su Shi (1037–1101 CE). Su Shi, also known as *Su Dongpo*, or 'Su-of-Eastern-Slope,' was born into a common family but passed the top tier of the *ke-ju* exams, attaining the highest offices before crashing to the ground after his outspoken attacks on the reform movement that had gained ascendancy at Court. Accused of treason—or as it was set out in Article 122 of the *Song Criminal Code*, 'Denouncing the Imperial Chariot'—Su was found guilty of treason at the famous 'Crow Terrace Trial' and exiled to a harsh and remote place in central China becoming an early victim of a government intent on crushing free speech. But great creativity is often stimulated by severe setbacks and hardship and Su's life was riven with difficulties that appears to have inspired his writing. He experienced the death of two wives whom he loved and also— heartbreakingly—the death of his fourth son as a baby boy.[1] Later, he was left moldering in exile tortured by his powerlessness to address the wrongs in society. His poetry can be useful in our own lives because he found the emotional balance necessary to cope with hardship and disappointment. Despite all of his difficulties, he achieved a detached tranquility, even light heartedness, by being able to accept that his troubles were just one part of the

---

1   One of the main reasons why I wanted to write this book is that I came across Su Shi's poem about the death of his infant son in a book by one of the masters of translation, Kenneth Roxreth. It felled me in my tracks. The death of a child is surely one of the worst experiences of a human life and Su Shi wrote about it in a particularly searing way by conjuring an image of the child and his former possessions that is almost unbearable. Roxreth had translated the second part of the poem and I wanted to know how Su Shi had felt about his wife, a mother shattered by the catastrophe. Since Chinese poems do not contain pronouns, I didn't know if he was writing about the calamity as 'me' or 'us.' I searched and searched and eventually found the whole of the original poem and, to my immense relief, I found that Su Shi has expressed profound sympathy towards his grieving wife by a direct reference rather than an ungendered pronoun. 母哭不可闻, he wrote: 'I cannot bear to hear his mother's sobs' or possibly 'His mother's sobs are inaudible'. I also found that he blamed his own sins for the disaster rather than the mother. I go back to this poem again and again. See page 129.

unfolding fate of the universe.

Su Shi was born in the south-western province of Sichuan during the rule of the Northern Song. He was a polymath—writer, poet, gastronome, pharmacologist, calligrapher and statesman. Both his brother and father were also famous literati. He passed the top-level *ke-ju* imperial exams at an unusually early age and thus attracted the attention of the emperor, attaining celebrity status after a brilliant exam performance requiring impromptu poetry composition. For twenty years, Su held a variety of government positions throughout China, notably in Hangzhou where he constructed a causeway across the West Lake, which is still there today and bears his name. In 1078 CE, he wrote a memorial describing problems in the local iron industry in Xuzhou and later a further memorial criticising Wang Anshi, a poet and powerful political rival also included later in this book. As a result, he was accused of treason, and after four months of evidence, the Censorate found him guilty, but commuted the sentence from death to exile. As a result, Su lost power and was sent to Huangzhou, a remote town in Hubei province on the Yangtse River, where he had no stipend and lived in poverty. With help from a friend, he built a small cottage on the eponymous 'Eastern Slope' and took to Buddhist meditation. It was in Huangzhou that Su Shi composed some of his best poems and painted his most famous calligraphy recording his state of desolate loneliness at the time of the Cold Food Festival.[1] In 1086 CE, he was recalled to court by a new administration, but was finally banished in 1094 CE to the remote southern city of Huizhou. Su Shi married three times, and each of his wives died during his lifetime. In common with most officials at that time, he was often separated from his family. He wrote movingly of his grief at the successive deaths of his wives and was buried by his younger brother next to his second wife. Su was vegetarian in the later stages of his life and wrote:

'Since my imprisonment I have not killed a single thing... having experienced such worry and danger myself, when I felt just like a fowl waiting in the kitchen, I can no longer bear to cause any living creature to suffer immeasurable fright and pain simply to please my palate.'[2]

Viewed through the lens of contemporary events, the key moment in Su Shi's life, the Crow Terrace Trial, could be seen as a struggle for free speech. The adverse verdict had the effect of dampening dissent at Court and it is not an exaggeration to say that its effects are still felt in Chinese society nearly a thousand years later.

1　See page 149.
2　自下狱后，念己亲经患难，不异鸡鸭之在庖厨，不欲使有生之类，受无量怖苦，遂断杀。

Li Qingzhao

Li Qingzhao (1084–c1151 CE) was born in present-day Shandong on the eastern coast of China to an aristocratic family which gave its daughters the same opportunities as its sons. Her father was a student of Su Shi, so she grew up in an atmosphere of erudition. Even before she was married in 1101 CE, her poems were well known. She appears to have enjoyed a happy marriage with a man of similarly enlightened views[1] and, although he was often away as an official, they shared an intellectual freedom and many artistic interests, and had a large collection of books, paintings, calligraphy, antiques and carvings. They also shared a love of poetry and often wrote poems for each other. In 1127 CE, the Northern Song fell to the Jurchens and their house was burned. Li fled southward to Nanjing, with the remnants of her possessions to join her husband there. However, in the midst of this turmoil, he died two years later, dealing her a blow from which she never fully recovered.

Li Qingzhao found herself in her mid-forties, stripped of the protections against the sexism of Song society—her husband, father and brothers dead, her great collection of art scattered to the four winds. Little is known of her last two decades and her

---

1   This has recently been contested.

later poetry displays a melancholy and a hatred of war, which is in sharp contrast to her earlier poems, which relate to her feelings as a young woman in love.[1] According to some accounts, Li made a second marriage to a man who treated her badly, so she divorced him, surviving the scandal and living in Hangzhou in relative poverty. From her voluminous writings, which extended to about a thousand poems in thirteen collections plus a collection of essays, only about fifty poems survive, but these are enough to cement her place as a major world poet.

Poetry in China is almost an exclusively male tradition, so Li Qingzhao deserves special attention. There were many female poets but few whose work survived to the present day. Women were generally literate, but from an early age tended to live in seclusion within closely watched family courtyards, which inevitably stunted the imagination and prevented women from enjoying the intellectual and artist freedom that men took for granted. There were exceptions; some families valued women as much as men, but more important was the resourcefulness shown by some women in escaping the fetters of society. Marriage in Song China—of course with notable exceptions—was generally a commercial arrangement between families and not, as in the

---

1 This is best illustrated by contrasting the poem about the sunset at Xiting Springs on page 191, which she wrote as a young woman, with the poem about the ice across her window on page 143, which she wrote in later life.

ideal in our own society, exclusive and founded on romantic love. Women were able to form relationships with married men that we would consider to be 'romantic,' in the sense that they derived from feelings rather than economic or political interests. It was, in those days, entirely normal for a man to have a relationship outside his marriage with a concubine or courtesan. These women were attractive not only for their looks, but also their intelligence, their conversation, their art, and through this, they were able to achieve economic independence. Thus they achieved also independence of spirit and there is evidence of a substantial body of poetry by women, much of which has not survived. Thankfully, Li Qingzhao's poetry is part of the surviving tradition and, I hope you will agree, she shines from the page.

Bizarrely, Li Qingzhao's name has been used by the International Astronomical Union (its Working Group for Planetary System Nomenclature, no less) to denote two impact craters caused by asteroids smashing into the southern hemisphere of Mercury and one other on the northern hemisphere of Venus. I am truly bamboozled by this bizarre piece of information and can't help wondering what she'd have make of it.

Lu You

Finally, we arrive in the company of Lu You (1125–1210 CE). Lu was only a few months old when the northern part of the

Song was lost and the capital moved southwards to Hangzhou. Until he was eight, Lu lived in poverty as a refugee from chaos before finally settling at his ancestor's farm in the south. Lu passed the *ke-ju* exams and, as an official, he strenuously advocated military confrontation with the invasion from the north. Thus he fell foul of the court, which was dominated by pacifists. Lu began to feel an intense frustration with his career and started to behave in a deliberately wild and reckless fashion, taking the literary name Fangweng, or 'Liberated Old Man.' He travelled extensively, moving from one minor post to another, several times being stripped of office for irresponsible behavior. Lu's poems are wide ranging and imaginative and, when he finally fell from office at the age of sixty-four, he retired to the same farm where he had lived as a boy and endured a life of increasing poverty. During his last twenty years, he wrote a poem every day. His writing grew into something more like a notebook or journal with concrete details of village life, the changing seasons and the different preoccupations of a human life as it moves through its different ages.

Lu You was born on a boat floating in the Wei River on a rainy morning on 17 October. Throughout his entire life, the country was threatened with invasion from the north after the Song Empire split into two. He died at eighty-six, having enjoyed excellent health due, so he claimed, to a diet of pearl barley and wood-ear mushrooms. He left an extraordinary body of work extending to over eleven thousand poems.

By twelve, Lu You was already an excellent writer and was interested in war strategy, having—like Li Bai—become an accomplished swordsman. He took the imperial exams at nineteen but failed. Ten years later, he graduated as the top scholar in the region, but could not progress further as he had attracted the spite of an untalented government official. It was not until after this official died that Lu You could take up his duties.

Lu You grew up with his cousin Tang Wan and they fell deeply in love, marrying at the age of twenty, but they had no children and Lu You's mother did not like his wife. Eventually, she forced Lu You to divorce her.[1] Eight years after the divorce, Lu You came across Tang Wan sitting in an ornamental garden together with her new husband. When she saw him, she came over with a cup of wine. As she passed it to him, he saw that her eyes were brimming with tears. Heartbroken, he drained the cup of bitter wine to the bottom. In the year before his death, at the age of eighty five, Lu wrote a poem called 'Shen's Garden' to commemorate Tang Wan and the spot where she had given him the wine nearly five decades earlier. Their story of enduring love is very famous in China.

In 1172 CE, Lu You started his official career as a strategic

---

1 Why didn't he just say 'No!'?

planner in the army. This gave him a chance of fulfilling his dream of seeing China reunited again and many of his poems reflect this patriotism. However, the Song Dynasty was by then corrupt and indolent so he had no opportunity fully to deploy his talents. Lu You felt there was no place for him in official life, and started to become self-indulgent, taking to drink to forget his lack of success in his personal life and career. Although he called himself 'Liberated Old Man,' he was sarcastic about himself in his poems. After several promotions and demotions, Lu You retired in 1190 CE to live in seclusion in his rural hometown. He spent the last twenty years of his life there until he died on January 26, 1210 CE.

11
If, Perhaps and Maybe

Faithful friends, those of you who have persevered with the journey, waded through tracts of Chinese history and struggled across the austere landscape of subatomic particles to get a taste of:

Up | Down | Strangeness | Charm | Beauty | Truth,

I have at last, and without any means of further prevarication, finally got to the point.

I want to take a Large Hadron Collider to seventy Chinese poems to smash them apart and see what lies inside them. I will scatter the Chinese characters so that we can watch their crackling traces pass across time and space. Rather than presenting individual specimens, I have sought to bring them all together in a contemporary voice—at least, I have tried to set them into the wider picture.

Whilst setting the poems into the six categories, I sensed a pattern emerge from the fog. The names of the first three quarks—

Introduction 前言

to me—suggest emotions that derive from struggle. 'Up' conjured images of the poets shouting in their drunken euphoria for ever increasing quantities of wine and battling with mania as they dance towards and then across the thin line between genius and madness; 'Down' is the struggle with sorrow, sorrow caused by the cruelty of nature and the cruelty of man, whilst 'Strangeness' suggests fear of the unknown or the unexplained, the struggle against nature in its weirdest forms—autumn gales, maggots, rats, locusts. Here the poets seem to taunt us by presenting the uncomfortable, ugly sides of the world through the strict constructs of classical poetry, and mocking us for believing that monks and prophets can show us the way to avoid our inevitable fate. The names of the second three quarks—'Charm,' 'Beauty' and 'Truth'—seem to point towards the relationship between each human being and other individuals, with nature and with society as a whole. 'Charm' speaks of the bonds of friendship and family; 'Beauty' alludes to the peace and comfort that can come from a sense of harmony with nature, whilst 'Truth' presents the unavoidable realities that bind individuals together and impose responsibilities towards society as a whole. But each of us can decide for ourselves which of these poems belongs in each of the six quark categories. Which, for you, is 'Up,' which has 'Charm' and which—for you—must be banished to 'Strangeness?'

Finally, I hope that we can stand back and share a sense of

common humanity as we gaze on the verses echoing down to us from these lives so distant in time and context from our own. If we can glimpse into the minds of these people who lived more than a thousand years ago and find familiarity, then perhaps, in a world that seems more fractious than ever, we may find more to bind us together than there is to set us apart.

Tim Clissold

认命斋

惊蛰　2021

Introduction　前言

Poems

诗歌

【 上 ｜ Up 】

noun: elevated mood, abnormal energy, euphoria, mania

derived from substance abuse, psyche or circumstance

adj: impulsive, precipitate, unrestrained

noun: ebullience, exuberance, excitability

adj: opposite of down

The spontaneity of the early Tang poets borders on the psychotic. Li Bai shouts hysterically: 'We must drink three hundred cups at once!' Later on, Lu You brings ruin on his family by reckless spending on three thousand stone jars of wine: 'Frenzied, I swept brushstrokes not knowing what I did,' he shouts, before pounding his fist into his mattress, howling into the void and covering the thirty foot wall of his room with wild, indecipherable characters. The fine line between genius and madness is crossed, so they seek oblivion instead: 'In the end, I don't even know I exist—that then is my greatest joy' writes Li Bai blind drunk again sometime in 745 CE—and elsewhere—'I only want to drink and never wake up!' But of course, they do wake up, hung over and bad-tempered after their excesses. We find them lolling around in bed all day long before finally getting up towards dusk. Without a hint of remorse, one writes 'I smile at my sloth and greed, since this bliss is all I know.' But finally they discover more lasting contentment: 'Apart from life's three pleasures,' writes Bai Juyi in 832 CE, 'the fourth is to play with my boy.'

初唐诗人的自发性介乎发狂的边缘。李白歇斯底里地狂吼："会须一饮三百杯！"不久后的陆游"倾家酿酒三千石""忽然挥扫不自知"，他大喊着，拳头重重地捶床（"槌床大叫狂堕帻"），在他房间的"三丈壁"上写满了难以辨认的狂草。天才与疯子的界线交错，于是他们转而寻求遗世。李白曾在公元 745 年某日又一次大醉而作"不知有吾身，此乐最为甚"，还曾道："但愿长醉不复醒。"他们当然会醒过来，只不过是带着放纵后的宿醉和暴躁。我们发现他们一整天都懒洋洋地待在床上，直到天黑才起来。但他们一点儿也不后悔，有人写道："慵馋还自哂，快活亦谁知。"不过最终他们还是找到了比醉酒更持久的满足感，公元 832 年白居易在一首诗中写道："荣公三乐外，仍弄小男儿。"

西江月

遣兴

辛弃疾

醉里且贪欢笑
要愁那得功夫
近来始觉古人书
信著全无是处

昨夜松边醉倒
问松我醉何如
只疑松动要来扶
以手推松曰去

West Moon River: Shouting Out My Feelings

Xin Qiji (1140–1207 CE)

In my drunkenness, I crave nothing but laughter—
    what's the point of feeling glum?
Recently I've been feeling that books by ancient masters
    are absolutely not to be trusted.

Last night I fell down by a pine
    and asked it 'How is my drunkenness!?'   105
I thought it was helping me up,
    so I pushed it and shouted 'Sod off!'

Up

上

将进酒

李白

君不见
黄河之水天上来
奔流到海不复回
君不见
高堂明镜悲白发
朝如青丝暮成雪
人生得意须尽欢
莫使金樽空对月
天生我材必有用
千金散尽还复来
烹羊宰牛且为乐
会须一饮三百杯
岑夫子　丹丘生
将进酒　杯莫停
与君歌一曲
请君为我倾耳听
钟鼓馔玉不足贵

Let's Drink Together!

Li Bai (701–762 CE)

Have you not seen—

　the Yellow River falls from Heaven,

　and, surging to the sea, never returns?

Have you not seen—

　in the mirrors in the Great Hall,

　hair that seemed so dark at dawn, by dusk had turned

　to snow?

107

For life to have meaning, we must strive for the limits of

happiness ,

　and never tip an empty glass to the moon.

The talent given to me by heaven must be put to good use.

If I risk a thousand gold pieces, they'll come back in the end,

　so—boil me a lamb! kill me an ox!—

　all shall celebrate.

We must drink three hundred cups at once!

Scholar Cen, Master Yuan—old friends—

Let's drink together, our cups must never stop!

And sing! All listen to my chant!

Bells, drums, jade—they are not fine enough for us.

Up

上

但愿长醉不复醒
古来圣贤皆寂寞
惟有饮者留其名
陈王昔时宴平乐
斗酒十千恣欢谑
主人何为言少钱
径须沽取对君酌
五花马　千金裘
呼儿将出换美酒
与尔同销万古愁

How many thinkers have been forgotten through the
ages?

Great drinkers are remembered more than sober sages;

I only want to drink and never wake up.

Take Prince Cao, feasting by Western Gate,

With fine wine and uproarious laughter,

How can our host complain about money?

Just fetch another barrel at once.

His horse with the plaited mane!

His furs of a thousand gold pieces!   109

Call the boy and have him swap them for fine wine and

    together you and I will wipe out the cares of ten thousand

    years.

草书歌行

李白

少年上人号怀素
草书天下称独步
墨池飞出北溟鱼
笔锋杀尽中山兔
八月九月天气凉
酒徒词客满高堂
笺麻素绢排数箱
宣州石砚墨色光
吾师醉后倚绳床
须臾扫尽数千张
飘风骤雨惊飒飒
落花飞雪何茫茫
起来向壁不停手
一行数字大如斗

Lines in Praise of Flowing Script

Li Bai (701–762 CE)

This young monk called Huaisu—

    his flowing script is unique.

Fish from the northern depths fly from his ink pool,

    a mountain full of rabbits

    were killed to make his brush.

In the eighth month, the ninth month, the weather grows cold;

    disciples of wine and verse crowd in the Great Hall.

Huaisu sets out boxes of fine paper and silks;

    ink glistens in his carved inkstone.

The Master, intoxicated, sits in his rope chair.

Then in an instant he has covered

    a thousand sheets of paper.

The room is filled with whirlwinds and driving rain,

    falling flowers and flying snow.

He stands, goes to the wall, and with a single sweep,

    brushes a line of characters as big as constellations.

Up
上

恍恍如闻神鬼惊
时时只见龙蛇走
左盘右蹙如惊电
状同楚汉相攻战
湖南七郡凡几家
家家屏障书题遍
王逸少　张伯英
古来几许浪得名
张颠老死不足数
我师此义不师古
古来万事贵天生
何必要公孙大娘浑脱舞

We hear the muddled voices of spirits and demons,

Dragons and snakes writhe before us,

    they coil to the left,

    they twist to the right

    like bolts of lightening

    or armies attacking each other in battle.

Noble families of the seven southern counties,

Sport your script on the screens by their gates.

Wang Xizhi! Zhang Boying!

    Your fame is utterly useless.

Crazy Zhang! You're not remotely in the same class.

Huaisu takes no lessons from these ancient masters.

Heaven-sent talent has always been admired,

    but now who needs a dance of whirling swords

    to inspire their sinuous script?

Up

上

草书歌

陆游

倾家酿酒三千石
闲愁万斛酒不敌
今朝醉眼烂岩电
提笔四顾天地窄
忽然挥扫不自知
风云入怀天借力
神龙战野昏雾腥
奇鬼摧山太阴黑
此时驱尽胸中愁
槌床大叫狂堕帻
吴笺蜀素不快人
付与高堂三丈壁

Calligraphy

Lu You (1125–1210 CE)

I brought ruin on my house by brewing three thousand jars,
   now ten thousand cups can't heal my deep dismay.
At dawn, my drunken eyes flashed as lightning down a cliff,
   I seized my brush and stared four-ways at the shrinking world
   around.
Frenzied, I swept brush strokes not knowing what I did,
   wind and clouds raged in my chest but heaven lent me
   strength.
I saw dragons fight in wastelands through dark mists that
stank of blood,
   strange ghosts toppled mountains and the moon turned
   icy black.

Suddenly all worry is driven from my mind—
   Madly I pound the bed and cry out as my cap comes
   tumbling down.
Fine paper and rare silks will not do for me,
   my verses must cover the thirty foot wall of this room.

115

Up

上

月下独酌（其一）

李白

花间一壶酒
独酌无相亲
举杯邀明月
对影成三人
月既不解饮
影徒随我身
暂伴月将影
行乐须及春
我歌月徘徊
我舞影零乱
醒时同交欢
醉后各分散
永结无情游
相期邈云汉

Drinking Alone Under the Moon (One)

Li Bai (701–762 CE)

Amongst the flowers, a pitcher of wine;

    alone I drink, no companion is here.

I raise my cup and invite the moon,

    with my shadow—well, that makes three!

But the moon is no drinker of wine,

    the shadow's steps cling to my own.

The moon's friendship; the company of my shadow—

I'll enjoy them both in the Spring.

I sing and the moon trails along,

I dance and my shadow's a whirl.

    When sober, we all share the fun,

    When drunk, we keep to ourselves.

Forever joined yet unattached old wanderers,

    let's meet where the universe ends.

Up 上

月下独酌（其二）

李白

天若不爱酒
酒星不在天
地若不爱酒
地应无酒泉
天地既爱酒
爱酒不愧天
已闻清比圣
复道浊如贤
贤圣既已饮
何必求神仙
三杯通大道
一斗合自然
但得醉中趣
勿为醒者传

Drinking Alone Under the Moon (Two)

Li Bai (701–762 CE)

If Heaven did not like wine,

there would be no such named star in the sky.

If Earth did not love wine,

no place would be named for its springs.

Since Heaven and Earth both love wine,

my drinking should not offend either.

119

Clear wine compares to a saint,

the dregs were once called a sage.

Both are talented drinkers,

what need do I have of a seer?

At the third cup, I see the transcendent;

a bottle, I'm "that which just is!"

Up

上

But these things that I sense when I'm drunk,

I will never disclose to the sober.

月下独酌（其三）

李白

三月咸阳城

千花昼如锦

谁能春独愁

对此径须饮

穷通与修短

造化夙所禀

一樽齐死生

万事固难审

醉后失天地

兀然就孤枕

不知有吾身

此乐最为甚

Drinking Alone Under the Moon (Three)

Li Bai (701–762 CE)

At the third moon, Xianyang town
   is spread with a carpet of flowers.
In Springtime, who wants to sit alone and mope?
I just go straight for the bottle.

Success or failure, long or short life,
Heaven allots each a share.
With a toast, life and death are the same
Wine makes things hard to explain.

When drunk, I lose Heaven and Earth —
   dazed, befuddled, inert, I grope for my solitary pillow.
   In the end, I don't know I exist —
   and that is my greatest joy!

晚起

白居易

烂熳朝眠后
频伸晚起时
暖炉生火早
寒镜裹头迟
融雪煎香茗
调酥煮乳糜
慵馋还自哂
快活亦谁知
酒性温无毒
琴声淡不悲
荣公三乐外
仍弄小男儿

Getting Up Late

Bai Juyi (772–846 CE)

Since dawn I lie here dissolute
   and stretch 'til I rise at dusk.
This evening the stove lights quickly,
   so I pause with my hair in the glass.

With tender leaves and melted snow,
I boil a fragrant tea;
   I cook a fine milk-pudding
   with flavoured curds and ghee.

I smile at my sloth and greed,
   since this bliss is all I know—
My wine is mild and harmless,
   my lute, it fills me with joy.
Apart from life's three pleasures,
   the fourth is to play with my boy.

Up
上

【 下 ∣ **Down** 】

noun: a turn for the worse, sorrow, worry, anxiety

adj: downcast, dejected, ailing, sick, grieving

adj: opposite of up

Whilst the excesses of 'Up' hint at a bipolar mind, 'Down' comes from a far saner disposition; but it is one paralysed by grief, suffering and loneliness rather than any innate or spontaneous depression. There is a reason for this sorrow. Su Shi writes of the death of his baby son: 'Why could we not have died with you? Your little clothes still hang on your rack, your milk still lies on the bed.' Later on, another seems stupefied by a double blow: 'Heaven's already taken my wife, now it's taken my son.' But this state of 'Down' comes not only from the cruelty of nature towards man but from man towards man. 'I can still cook the morning gruel,' pleads an old woman offering herself up to the pressgang in a desperate ploy to protect her grandson from the draft. She had already lost two out of three sons and, after this encounter with the soldiers, she dies overnight from grief and worry: 'Deep in the night, her voice grew still, dim echoes of choking sobs.' Suffering infuses these poems, but the final resilient voice—that of the poetess Li Qingzhao who wrote whilst mourning her dead husband 'Better to drown my sorrows, than disappoint the chrysanthemums that lean on the eastern fence'—shows that the best defence against disaster is loyalty and companionship.

如果说"上"暗示着双相情感思维，那么"下"则夹带着更多的理性。然而这份愁更多的是遭受悲伤、痛苦和孤独而造成的，并非天性忧郁或是自发抑郁。这份忧愁往往都有原因。苏轼在小儿子夭折时曾写道："欲与汝俱亡。故衣尚悬架，涨乳已流床。"而不久之后另一位诗人更是遭到双重打击："天既丧我妻，又复丧我子"。但这份愁绪不只来源于自然对人的残酷，还来自于人与人之间。一位为了保护膝下乳孙免受征兵之害的老奶奶，自愿以自己的老迈身躯为军队"犹得备晨炊"。这位妇人已经失去了三个儿子中的两个，再遇这次官吏"捉人"，老妇竟一夜之间因悲伤和惊惧过度而离开了人世："夜久语声绝，如闻泣幽咽"。这些诗歌充满了苦难，但最后却有一种坚忍的声音，诗人李清照在思念死去的丈夫时写道："不如随分尊前醉，莫负东篱菊蕊黄，"表明忠诚与陪伴是对抗苦难最好的办法。

去岁九月二十七日，在黄州，生子遁，小名干儿，颀然颖异。至今年七月二十八日，病亡于金陵，作二诗哭之

苏轼

吾年四十九

羁旅失幼子

幼子真吾儿

眉角生已似

未期观所好

蹁跹逐书史

摇头却梨栗

似识非分耻

吾老常鲜欢

赖此一笑喜

忽然遭夺去

恶业我累尔

Two poems of tears written after the death of my son named Dun, and nicknamed Gan, born last year in Huangzhou on the twenty-seventh day of the ninth month (12 September, 1083 CE) and imposingly unique until he died of illness in Jinling this year on the twenty-eighth day of the seventh month (31 August, 1084 CE), aged one.

Su Shi (1037–1101 CE)

In my forty-ninth year, whilst travelling,

    I lost an infant.

That infant was indeed my son.

    His brows already like mine,

Not one year old, I watched with such delight,

    tottering towards my books of histories and poems.

He'd shake his head, refusing pears and chestnuts

    as if he thought he wasn't worthy.

He gave me such a vital joy,

    I relied on him for all my daily laughter.

Suddenly he was torn from us,

    I blame my sins for this catastrophe.

Down 下

衣薪那免俗

变灭须臾耳

归来怀抱空

老泪如泻水

我泪犹可拭

日远当日忘

母哭不可闻

欲与汝俱亡

故衣尚悬架

涨乳已流床

感此欲忘生

一卧终日僵

中年忝闻道

梦幻讲已详

储药如丘山

临病更求方

仍将恩爱刃

割此衰老肠

知迷欲自反

一恸送余伤

So small, his firewood shroud refutes all natural law,

    snuffed out he is, and that's the end of it.

I return home to find but an empty embrace,

    my tears are like the shits, ungovernable.

These tears of mine must be wiped away endlessly,

    the time is far off when I'll forget this terrible day.

I cannot bear to hear his mother's sobs—

    why could we not have died with you?

Your little clothes still hang on your rack,

    your milk still lies on the bed.

In such anguish, we forget our own lives,

    lying all day prostrate, insensible.

I'm too old to understand what has happened,

    but foresaw it all in a dream.

Medicine heaped high as mountains,

    yet we found no effective prescription.

I'll take a sword forged from this thwarted love,

    and cut out my guts from the waist.

I am lost—but must come to my senses—

    Tho' this wound will grieve me forever.

捣练子

李煜

深院静　小庭空
断续寒砧断续风
无奈夜长人不寐
数声和月到帘栊

云鬟乱　晚妆残
带恨眉儿远岫攒
斜托香腮春笋嫩
为谁和泪倚阑干

The Washerwoman's Lament

Li Yu (937–978 CE)

Deep in the courtyard all is still, the hall is empty now;
    when she beats her clothes on the ancient block,
    the wind gusts cold around.

Night wears on, but no one yet can sleep;
    as moonbeams mix with voices,
    at the curtained window above.

Dishevelled cloud-like hair, her nightdress hangs undone;
    eyebrows arch like the far-off hills,
    cheeks slant as she leans on her hand.

Down　下

She broods on distant memories, still tender as shoots in
the Spring;
    for whom does she know these tears,
    as she leans on the balustrade?

秋夜闻雨三首

朱淑真

似箭撩风穿帐幕
如倾凉雨咽更筹
冷怀敧枕人无寐
铁石肝肠也泪流

竹窗萧索镇如秋
雨滴檐花夜不休
独宿广寒多少恨
一时分付我心头

似篾身材无事瘦
如丝肠肚怎禁愁
鸣窗更听芭蕉雨
一叶中藏万斛愁

Listening to the Rain on an Autumn Night

Zhu Shuzhen (c1135–c1180 CE)

The wind, like an arrow, pierces the curtains round my bed,
   slanting rain sobs icy through the night.
My breasts are freezing as I lie sleepless on my pillow,
   guts clogged with iron stones, my tears flow freely down.

Wind sighs in the bamboo, pressing like a doleful autumn,
   rain splatters the patterned eaves
   on through this ceaseless night.
Alone, I count my regrets in this sprawling, frigid room—
   it seems as if I am losing my mind!

Bored and with nothing to do, I'm as frail as a bamboo strip,
   my bowels, thin as threads,
   how can they stand this strain?
I hear the rain on the plantain by my window,
   each leaf stores a thousand sorrows.

Down 下

石壕吏

杜甫

暮投石壕村
有吏夜捉人
老翁逾墙走
老妇出门看
吏呼一何怒
妇啼一何苦
听妇前致词
三男邺城戍
一男附书至
二男新战死
存者且偷生
死者长已矣
室中更无人
惟有乳下孙

The Pressgang at Stone Moat

Du Fu (712–770 CE)

At dusk in Stone Moat Village,

    the pressgang came to seize men.

An old one hopped over the wall,

    his wife at the door looked on.

What fury in the shouts of the officers!

    how bitter the old woman's sobs!

Yet I heard her opening words—

    "Three men of this house at the borders

        one of them sent me a note—

    the others just killed in the war.

Two dead now gone forever,

    —the last on borrowed time.

At home there's nobody left,

    save a grandson still on the breast.

Down 下

有孙母未去
出入无完裙
老妪力虽衰
请从吏夜归
急应河阳役
犹得备晨炊
夜久语声绝
如闻泣幽咽
天明登前途
独与老翁别

His mother never remarried,

    her clothes, in tatters, hang open.

Tho' my strength has failed

    I will go with you in the night.

I can still cook the morning gruel

    so I'll join your Heyang draft."

Deep in the night, her voice grew still,

    dim echoes of choking sobs.

At dawn when I started my journey,

    the old man was left all alone.

139

Down 下

书哀

梅尧臣

天既丧我妻
又复丧我子
两眼虽未枯
片心将欲死
雨落入地中
珠沉入海底
赴海可见珠
掘地可见水
唯人归泉下
万古知已矣
拊膺当问谁
憔悴鉴中鬼

Writing of My Sorrow

Mei Yaochen (1002–1060 CE)

Heaven's already taken my wife,
  now it's taken my son.
My eyes are still not cried out,
  my heart yearns only for death.

Rain soaks into the ground,
  pearls may sink to the ocean depths.
But—
  Dive in the sea and you might find a pearl,
  Scoop out the earth and you may find water.

Only people return to their source, irretrievably—
  as we've known from the beginning of time.

Beating my chest; to whom can I turn?
  —all haggard and wan like a ghost in my mirror.

Down 下

鹧鸪天

李清照

寒日萧萧上琐窗
梧桐应恨夜来霜
酒阑更喜团茶苦
梦断偏宜瑞脑香

秋已尽　日犹长
仲宣怀远更凄凉
不如随分尊前醉
莫负东篱菊蕊黄

Partridge Sky

Li Qingzhao (1084–c1151 CE)

The icy sun climbs mournfully across the lattice of my window,

the phoenix tree suffers the frost that comes by night.

I finish my wine and take my bitter tea,

lay by my dreams as the scent ascends to my head.

Autumn is already over, yet the day still seems long,

thinking of hometown, I'm pierced with a stinging

cold—

Better to drown my sorrows, than disappoint the

chrysanthemums,

that lean on Eastern Fence.

【 奇 ∣ Strangeness 】

noun: the quality or condition of being strange by unusual,
new or otherwise fascinating characteristics
adj (strange) : unusual, curious, odd, bewildering
noun: monster, demon, evil being, goblin

Strangeness speaks of the darker, more threatening side of nature. Famished rats gnaw on books, locusts lay eggs on a soldier's corpse. An exiled poet has nothing but damp weeds for his stove in winter and louts run off with Du Fu's thatched roof blown off by autumn gales. By focusing on the unpleasant—the disgusting—through the medium of verse, the poets mock our sensibilities. One almost dares us not to vomit when he describes crows tugging at maggots: 'Rat carcass breakfasts are few and far between,' he says, 'so they come to peck at maggots in the filth of the latrine.' Elsewhere, we see inexplicable events, like the lunar eclipse that sends Mei Yaochen's wife scurrying to 'fry round cakes' and his son 'banging on (round) mirrors.' Attempts to avoid nature's grim march prove futile; Han Yu's teeth fall out, Bai Juyi goes bald. And yet, even after incessant rain, surrounded by fat fungus, earthworms, mold and frogs, Mei Yaochen finds comfort in the companionship of his wife. Unlike the wife of Bo Lun, the legendary drunkard who shunned all social convention, Mei's wife stayed by his side even whilst he was blind drunk. In the end, the best armour against fear is friendship.

"奇"指的是大自然更黑暗、更具威胁性的一面。饥饿的老鼠啃噬书本，蝗虫在士兵的尸体上产卵，被贬谪的诗人在冬天火炉里除了潮湿的杂草什么都没有，杜甫茅屋的屋顶也被秋风吹掉了，还有一群男孩抢了茅草跑了。诗人们通过诗歌这一媒介把注意力集中在令人不快的，甚至是令人厌恶的事物上，从而嘲弄人类的情感。当诗人描述乌鸦啄蛆时，那幅画面也不怕我们吐出来，他写道："岂无腐鼠食，来啄秽厕虫。"我们还在别处看到一些令人费解的事，比如月食的出现让梅尧臣的妻子忙着"煎饼去"，他的儿子忙着"敲镜"。企图避开大自然的严酷规律更是徒劳的，韩愈的牙掉了，白居易的头发也掉光了。然而，即便阴雨连绵，菌类肥、蚯蚓长、蛤蟆闹，梅尧臣仍在妻子的陪伴下找到了慰藉。不像传说中的伯伦——一个毫不在意社会习俗的酒鬼的妻子，梅尧臣的妻子即便在他酩酊大醉的时候依然陪伴在他身边，这证明情谊是抵御恐惧最好的盔甲。

寒食雨二首

苏轼

自我来黄州
已过三寒食
年年欲惜春
春去不容惜
今年又苦雨
两月秋萧瑟
卧闻海棠花
泥污燕脂雪
暗中偷负去
夜半真有力
何殊病少年
病起头已白

春江欲入户
雨势来不已
小屋如渔舟
蒙蒙水云里
空庖煮寒菜
破灶烧湿苇

Rain at Cold Food Festival

Su Shi (1037–1101 CE)

Since I came to Huangzhou,
  already three Cold-food Festivals have passed.
Each year I cherish the springtime,
  but it departs without a care.
This year again the rain is exhausting,
  months of dreary autumn-like weather.
Lying in bed, I listen to the showers on the crab-apple blossom,
  their petals fall down to the mire.
Secretly the Spring steals away,
  wilful in the dead of the night.
How is it different from a sickly youth,
  rising from his bed, hair already white?

The Spring river wants to pour through my window,
  the force of the rain is unrelenting.
My small house is like a little fishing boat,
  amid a fog of clouds and water.
In an empty kitchen I boil cold vegetables,
  in a broken stove I burn wet weeds.

Strangeness 奇

那知是寒食
但见乌衔纸
君门深九重
坟墓在万里
也拟哭涂穷
死灰吹不起

Poems
诗
歌

How would I know that today is the Cold-food Festival

    if it wasn't for ravens with paper money in their beaks?

The emperor's gates are nine layers deep,

    the family tombs ten thousand miles away.

Will I just sit and weep at my endless exhaustion?

    dead ashes won't blow back to life.

151

Strangeness 奇

同谢师厚宿胥氏书斋，闻鼠，甚患之

梅尧臣

灯青人已眠

饥鼠稍出穴

掀翻盘盂响

惊聒梦寐辍

唯愁几砚扑

又恐架书啮

痴儿效猫鸣

此计诚已拙

Staying Overnight with Xie Shihou in the Xu Family Library and Being Bothered by Hearing Rats

Mei Yaochen (1002–1060 CE)

The lantern's grown dark and all are asleep,

As famished rats poke hesitantly from their holes.

Startled by the din of tumbling cups and plates,

My dream comes to an end at once.

I worry they'll knock the ink stone from the table,

Or gnaw at books on the shelves.

Now my imbecile boy starts mewing like a cat.

Honestly! What a stupid idea.

Strangeness 奇

八月九日晨兴如厕，有鸦啄蛆

梅尧臣

飞乌先日出
谁知彼雌雄
岂无腐鼠食
来啄秽厕虫
饱腹上高树
跂觜噪西风
吉凶非予闻
臭恶在尔躬
物灵必自絜
可以推始终

Poems 诗歌

Waking up on Ninth August and Going to the Latrine Only to Find Crows Pecking at Maggots

Mei Yaochen (1002–1060 CE)

Before the rising sun, the birds swoop and whirl,
    featureless and uniform, which is boy or girl?

Rat carcass breakfasts are few and far between,
    so they come to peck at maggots in the filth of the latrine.

155

With a bellyful they're off and land up high in trees,
    and caw with raucous beaks at the early western breeze.

Auspicious or ferocious, I cannot tell;
Odorous! Malevolent! They fly at you from hell—

but the Spirit of all Things must make its own self pure,
    and find, from start to finish, the means to endure.

普净院佛阁上孤鹘

梅尧臣

我新税居见寺阁
金碧照我破屋前
目看阁上聚鸠鸽
巢栖饮哺忘穷年
雕檐画壁屎污遍
以及像塑头与肩
寺僧不敢施弹射
忽有苍鹘张毒拳
鸦鸣鹊噪鸠鸽叫
怒鹘来此窥腥膻
鹘心决裂不畏众
臀碎一脑惊后先

Lone Raptor on the Temple of Universal Purity

Mei Yaochen (1002–1060 CE)

I can see the temple pavilion from my newly rented shack,

    its blue and gold reflect on the crumbling walls around.

Turtle-doves and pigeons gather high on the towering roof,

    nesting, perching, feeding, they forget the year has an end.

Carved eaves, painted walls, but shit splattered everywhere,

    even on the heads of the Buddha statues below.

Yet the monks still dare not fire their crossbow darts.

Suddenly, an ash-grey raptor spreads its cruel and terrible claws.

Crows shriek, the magpies cry, a mynah bird squawks and squeals,

    whilst on high, the fearsome executioner hovers,

    peeking at fresh meat, sniffing the scent of death.

It measures; it decides; outnumbered, yet it fears no gathering crowd—

    then in a flash, the first brain-case smashed to pap,

    terror runs through the flock from end to end.

157

Strangeness 奇

死鸟堕空未及地
返翅下取如风旋
独当屋脊恣扯磔
啄肉披肝肠弃捐
老鸱无艺又狠怯
盘飞欲近饥目穿
逡巡鹊饱自飞去
争残不辨乌与鸢
群儿指点路人笑
我方吟忆秋江边

Corpse plummets through the wind but never hits the
ground—

    pivoting on a wing, the falcon grabs it mid-air.

It settles alone on the roof, tears open the ribs with relish,

    gulps down hunks, slashes up the liver, spits the

    intestines away.

Scavengers, artless and timid, circle resentfully above,

    desperate to get close, eyes stare hungrily down,

    they cower as the glutted killer once more takes to wing.

Then in a frenzy, they tear at the remains,

    no telling each bird apart.

159

Urchins point up and gawp; passers on the road just laugh;

    and I keep chanting the same old songs on the banks of the

    autumn stream.

Strangeness

奇

月蚀

梅尧臣

有婢上堂来
白我事可惊
天如青玻璃
月若黑水精
时当十分圆
只见一寸明
主妇煎饼去
小儿敲镜声
此虽浅近意
乃重补救情
夜深桂兔出
众星随西倾

Lunar Eclipse

Mei Yaochen (1002–1060 CE)

A maid comes rushing into the house
  interrupting me with shocking reports.

"The sky has turned to turquoise glass,
  the moon fused black as quartz.
It should be quite round right now,
  but it's just a sliver of light!"

My wife hurries off to fry round cakes,
  my son starts banging on mirrors.
This might show a rather shallow mindset,
  but they just want to get back to normal.

As night deepens, the moon reappears,
  and draws the stars to the West.

Strangeness 奇

落齿

韩愈

去年落一牙
今年落一齿
俄然落六七
落势殊未已
余存皆动摇
尽落应始止
忆初落一时
但念豁可耻
及至落二三
始忧衰即死
每一将落时
懔懔恒在已
叉牙妨食物
颠倒怯漱水
终焉舍我落
意与崩山比
今来落既熟
见落空相似
余存二十余
次第知落矣

My Falling Teeth

Han Yu (768–824 CE)

Last year, a tooth fell straight out,

    this year another one too.

Six or seven are ready to leave me,

    this dwindling's not going to cease.

The rest of them wobble inside me,

    it'll end when they've all fallen out.

I recall when I lost the first molar,

    I felt so ashamed of the gap.

Two more were on their way out,

    It's surely a sign of my death.

Each time one starts to get looser,

    I quiver and shiver with dread.

Forked teeth are no good for eating,

    but gargling would wash them all out.

In the end, I'll lose the whole mouthful,

    My spirits—like mountains—will fall.

I guess I'll finally get used to it,

    each gap is just like the next.

There are twenty more left at the moment,

    one by one they will go their own way.

163

Strangeness

奇

倘常岁一落
自足支两纪
如其落并空
与渐亦同指
人言齿之落
寿命理难恃
我言生有涯
长短俱死尔
人言齿之豁
左右惊谛视
我言庄周云
木雁各有喜
语讹默固好
嚼废软还美
因歌遂成诗
持用诧妻子

If each year one falls, I suppose,

    I'll last two decades at least.

Really, it won't make much difference,

    if they fall out all at one time.

They say that once your teeth loosen,

    one can't say how long you will last.

But I say that each life has limits,

    in the end, each of us dies.

When people examine my molars,

    they are shocked to see gaps right and left.

But I just quote the old story,

    that all things are useful in time.

When slurring it's best to keep silent,

    can't chew but soft things taste fine.

So I'll sing out this jovial poem,

    to impress both my children and wife.

165

Strangeness 奇

师厚云虱古未有诗，邀予赋之

梅尧臣

贫衣弊易垢
易垢少虱难
群处裳带中
旅升裘领端
藏迹讵可索
食血以自安
人世犹俯仰
尔生何足观

Xie Shihou Says the Ancient Masters Never Wrote a Poem about Lice so Why Don't I Write One

Mei Yaochen (1002–1060 CE)

Poor clothes get dirty,

Grime comes easy and lice do too.

Gathering in the folds at the belt,

Wandering through fur up my collar.

Hidden so tight, who can find them?

Slurping all peaceful and snug.

A man's life is gone in an instant,

So what's in the life of a louse?

167

Strangeness

奇

嗟发落

白居易

朝亦嗟发落
暮亦嗟发落
落尽诚可嗟
尽来亦不恶
既不劳洗沐
又不烦梳掠
最宜湿暑天
头轻无髻缚
脱置垢巾帻
解去尘缨络
银瓶贮寒泉
当顶倾一勺
有如醍醐灌
坐受清凉乐
因悟自在僧
亦资于剃削

Oh No! My Hair's Falling Out.

Bai Juyi (772–846 CE)

At dawn, I sigh at thin wisps,

    they fall out and at night it's the same.

I dread when the last lock will leave me,

    but once gone I don't mind at all.

I have done with the washing and drying,

    my comb is forever set by.

When the weather is hot and it's raining,

    there's no topknot to weigh down my head.

I have discarded my messy cloth wrappings,

    I've got rid of my dusty old fringe.

In a pitcher I store some cold water,

    and ladle it over my head.

It's like I'm baptised by the Buddha,

    and sit in his cool cleansing bliss.

And all of the monks there who praise him,

    have already shaved their own heads!

Strangeness 奇

茅屋为秋风所破歌

杜甫

八月秋高风怒号

卷我屋上三重茅

茅飞度江洒江郊

高者挂罥长林梢

下者飘转沉塘坳

南村群童欺我老无力

忍能对面为盗贼

公然抱茅入竹去

唇焦口燥呼不得

归来倚杖自叹息

俄顷风定云墨色

秋天漠漠向昏黑

布衾多年冷似铁

骄儿恶卧踏里裂

床头屋漏无干处

雨脚如麻未断绝

Lines on the Damage to My Thatched Cottage Caused by Autumn Gales

Du Fu (712–770 CE)

Autumn winds rage early—

    three layers off my old thatched roof.

Straw flies over the river, scattered about on the banks;

    high reeds hang up on branches,

    low ones twirl in the ditch.

Kids from the village prey on my age,

    stealing from under my nose.

They cart off my roof to the bamboo glade;

    lips parched, mouth dry, I can barely utter a word.

I lean on my stick and heave a wretched sigh.

The wind soon drops, skies turn inky black,

    autumn dusk fades in the darkening night.

My tattered quilt is old, it feels as cold as iron,

    my restless boy kicks holes in the threadbare cloth.

The roof is leaking buckets and nowhere's slightly dry—

    rain falls dense as hemp, when will it ever cease?

Strangeness

奇

自经丧乱少睡眠

长夜沾湿何由彻

安得广厦千万间

大庇天下寒士俱欢颜

风雨不动安如山

呜呼　何时眼前突兀见此屋

吾庐独破受冻死亦足

Since the chaos of the rebellion, I've had so little sleep;

    soaked all night, how can I get to the end?

If only I had a house with a thousand rooms,

    to shelter poor scholars, living together in joy.

Steady as a mountain, unmoved by wind and rain,

if this great house appeared before my eyes,

    I'd willingly die of cold,

    in my wretched straw-thatched hut.

Strangeness 奇

蝗飞高

徐照

战士尸上虫
虫老生翅翼
目怒体甲硬
岂非怨气激
栉栉北方来
横遮遍天黑
戍妇闻我言
色变气咽逆
良人近战死
尸骸委砂砾
昨夜魂梦归
白骑晓无迹
因知天中蝗
乃是尸上物
仰面久迎视
低头泪双滴
呼儿勿杀害
解系从所适
蝗乎若有知
飞入妾心臆

Poems
诗
歌

The Locusts Fly High

Xu Zhao (?–1211 CE)

Locusts laid eggs on the soldier's corpse—
　　as worms matured, they sprouted wings.
Eyes of rage, shells hard and stiff,
　　who would not detest that furious swarm?
Packed close, they come woven together,
　　a blot on the sky, inky black.

When the garrison wife heard of his fate,
　　she paled, breath caught in her throat.
Her good-man killed in battle,
　　bones heaped like gravel stones.

Last night in a cloud-spirit dream,
　　riding aimlessly 'til dawn without tracks.
High up she'd seen locusts and knew they'd fed on
the dead—
　　raised her head and thought of a life without age,
　　then lowered with a pair of bitter tears.
Thereafter she would never let her children harm an insect,
　　but lift her head to the sky and cry out,
　　"Locusts, if you need it,
　　you may fly into my heart for shelter."

Strangeness 奇

梅雨

梅尧臣

三日雨不止
蚯蚓上我堂
湿菌生枯篱
润气醭素裳
东池虾蟆儿
无限相跳梁
野草侵花圃
忽与栏干长
门前无车马
苔色何苍苍
屋后昭亭山
又被云蔽藏
四向不可往
静坐唯一床
寂然忘外虑
微诵黄庭章
妻子笑我闲
曷不自举觞
已胜伯伦妇
一醉犹在傍

Plum Rain

Mei Yaochen (1002–1060 CE)

Three days, and the rain never ceases,
   the earthworms, they squirm in my room.
Wet fungus grows fat on dry fences,
   damp air brings white mold to my clothes.
In East Pond—green frogs—they are leaping,
   jumping over and over again.
The reeds are invading my garden,
   in a blink, they're as high as my fence.
At my gate, there's no horse and no carriage,
   the moss grows so thick and so green.
Behind me, Bright Pergola Mountain,
   is veiled with thick clouds once again.
I can't travel in any direction,
   I lie calm and alone on my bed.
Serenely, I shed all my worries,
   chanting verses there under my breath.
My wife, she laughs at my languor,
   "Raise a cup to yourself!" she exclaims.
So much for the wife of Bo Lun—
   I'm smashed but mine still remains.

Strangeness 奇

〖 魅 ∣ Charm 〗

noun: a power of pleasing or attracting

verb: to delight or please greatly by generosity, humour,

honesty, faithfulness or grace, to enchant

as if with a compelling or magical force

'Charm' takes us through the shifting nature of friendship, love and family. It traces our progress through life and maps the changing qualities in our relationships as we age. We start with courtship; two adolescents have been sent to Five Lakes to gather rushes for thatching. 'You and I in the same boat... At dawn, we left Orchid Island, paused under mulberry and elm. You and I plucking rushes, not a handful gathered by dusk!' Then the age of desire: 'Hurry up, young Master, to bed!' she says. 'All at once, I put down my needle, slip my gown, with a lust I can't curb.' Next the all-absorbing task of rearing children, where we find Mei Yaochen making excuses for not visiting a friend: 'Both clutch my clothes, tottering after every step. I just can't make it to the door, wrapped in this unmoveable love.' And in later life, the comfort of lasting friendships: 'Tonight then is a rare event, together you and I in the candlelight. We were young and lusty not so long ago, (but) now grown grey at the temples,' writes Du Fu on a reunion after twenty years. And then separation: 'Enjoy the springtime with all your strength,' says General Su Wu leaving for battle. 'And think of the days we were happy. If I live, I will come back— if I die, remember me always.'

"魅"带我们历经友谊、爱情与家庭的变迁。它记录了我们人生的进程，描绘了随着年龄增长，我们人际关系中不断变化的实质。让我们从求爱开始：两个青年前往"五湖"拔蒲草，"与君同舟去……朝发桂兰渚，昼息桑榆下。与君同拔蒲，竟日不成把"。接着便是情欲时代："催促少年郎，先去睡"，"须臾放了残针线，脱罗裳恣情无限"。之后便是抚养孩子的重担，这亦成为梅尧臣不去拜访朋友的借口："牵裳步步随。出门虽不远，情爱未能移"。到了晚年生活，长久的友谊成了慰藉，杜甫在二十年后的一次友人聚会时写道："今夕复何夕，共此灯烛光。少壮能几时，鬓发各已苍。"然后则是别离，苏武将军奔赴战场前写道："努力爱春华，莫忘欢乐时。生当复来归，死当长相思。"

拔蒲

佚名

青蒲衔紫茸
长叶复从风
与君同舟去
拔蒲五湖中
朝发桂兰渚
昼息桑榆下
与君同拔蒲
竟日不成把

Poems 诗歌

Plucking the Rushes

Anonymous

Green stems, red shoots in my teeth,
Long leaves that bend to the wind—
You and I in the same boat,
Plucking rushes at Five Lakes.

At dawn, we left Orchid Island,
Paused under mulberry and elm.
You and I plucking rushes,
Not a handful gathered by dusk.

183

Charm

魅

花非花

白居易

花非花
雾非雾
夜半来
天明去
来如春梦几多时
去似朝云无觅处

A Flower That Is No Flower

Bai Juyi (772–846 CE)

A flower that is no flower,

In fog that is not fog.

At midnight she'll come,

As the dawn lights, she goes.

Here like a Spring dream, how long will she stay?

Gone like clouds in the morning, never to be seen again.

185

Charm

魅

无题

李商隐

相见时难别亦难
东风无力百花残
春蚕到死丝方尽
蜡炬成灰泪始干
晓镜但愁云鬓改
夜吟应觉月光寒
蓬山此去无多路
青鸟殷勤为探看

Poems 诗歌

Untitled

Li Shangyin (c813–c858 CE)

We met with awkward blushes, but parting's harder still,
　　as eastern winds blow soft and a hundred petals fade.
Cocoons lie dead once their silken threads are spun,
　　like candles burned to ash whose teardrops start to dry.

Sadness stares from the morning mirror
　　as she tends her tangled hair.
His sighs last through the sleepless nights
　　as moonlight chills the air.
Their love lies on an imaginary hill, not far—
　　yet only birds can reach it.

187

Charm

魅

菊花新

柳永

欲掩香帏论缱绻

先敛双蛾愁夜短

催促少年郎

先去睡

鸳衾图暖

须臾放了残针线

脱罗裳恣情无限

留取帐前灯

时时待

看伊娇面

To the Tune of New Chrysanthemum Flowers

Liu Yong (c987–c1053 CE)

We ache to draw the bed curtains,
  and frown that the night's too short.
"Hurry up, young Master, to bed
  and warm the duck quilt for me!"

All at once, I put down my needle,
  slip my gown, with a lust I can't curb.
"But don't dim the light yet," —he pauses—
  "first a glimpse of your adorable face. "

189

Charm

魅

如梦令

李清照

常记溪亭日暮
沉醉不知归路
兴尽晚回舟
误入藕花深处
争渡　争渡
惊起一滩鸥鹭

Lines from a Dream

Li Qingzhao (1084–c1151 CE)

I often think of the pavilion by the brook,
    against the setting sun.
So drunk we were, we could not find our way home.
Then once our ecstasy was spent, we turned the boat
    t'wards evening,
        and blundered on a tangle of lotus flowers.
Straining through, straining through —
    we startled a shoreline of gulls.

191

Charm

魅

长干行

李白

妾发初覆额
折花门前剧
郎骑竹马来
绕床弄青梅
同居长干里
两小无嫌猜
十四为君妇
羞颜未尝开
低头向暗壁
千唤不一回
十五始展眉
愿同尘与灰
常存抱柱信
岂上望夫台
十六君远行
瞿塘滟滪堆

Leaving Longbank Village

Li Bai (701–762 CE)

When my girlish hair first covered my brows,

    I was plucking at flowers by the gate.

You rode by on a bamboo horse,

    toying with plums in your hands.

We lived in Longbank Village,

    infants with no glimmer of doubt.

When I was fourteen, I became your wife,   193

    so bashful, I never smiled,

Just lowered my head by the wall.

You called a thousand times, but I never came,

    yet at fifteen, my face relaxed—

I wished to be with you always,

    like dust mixed up with ash.

I trust that you will come back,

    no need for a watchtower to pine.

At sixteen, you travelled afar,

    to the Dyke of Rippling Waves.

Charm 魅

五月不可触
猿声天上哀
门前迟行迹
一一生绿苔
苔深不能扫
落叶秋风早
八月蝴蝶黄
双飞西园草
感此伤妾心
坐愁红颜老
早唤下三巴
预将书报家
相迎不道远
直至长风沙

I have not been able to feel you for five long months 'til now,

    whilst mournful shrieks of apes rise to the gloomy skies.

Your loitering feet left footprints by the gate,

    where moss grows thick and even, green as green can be.

So deep it grows—the moss—I cannot sweep it clean,

    the leaves blow there in autumn, in a blustery early breeze.

By the eighth moon, butterflies turn to gold,

    fluttering in pairs on the lawn,

    reminding me of my sorrow, as I grow ruddy and old.

If you sail downstream from the West,

    send a letter ahead to our home.

I still long to greet you—

    so I'll trek to Long Wind Sands.

195

Charm

魅

将赴表臣会呈杜挺之

梅尧臣

莫怪去迟迟

予心君亦知

膝前娇小女

眼底宁馨儿

学语渠渠问

牵裳步步随

出门虽不远

情爱未能移

An Excuse for Not Returning the Visit of a Friend

Mei Yaochen (1002–1060 CE)

Do not be offended if I refuse—

    you know me too well for that.

On my lap sits my precious girl,

    by my knee stands my handsome boy.

He's just begun to talk,

    and asks me questions without cease.

Both clutch my clothes, tottering after every step.

I just can't make it to the door,

    wrapped in this unmoveable love.

197

Charm

魅

夜出偏门还三山

陆游

月行南斗边
人归西郊路
水风吹葛衣
草露湿芒履
渔歌起远汀
鬼火出破墓
凄清醒醉魂
荒怪入诗句
到家夜已半
伫立叩蓬户
稚子犹读书
一笑慰迟暮

Setting out to Return to Three Hills at Night

Lu You (1125–1210 CE)

The moon so high, near Southern Lights,

    I return by the road from the west.

Damp breeze ruffles my poplin coat,

    dew from the grass soaks my shoes.

Fishermen's songs drift on sandflats,

    fires dance ghostly on tombs.

Chill winds soon make me sober,

    strange thoughts in my mind unrestrained.

At home when the night is half over,

    I stand at my tumbleweed door.

Upstairs my nipper's still reading —

    one laugh, all my troubles consoled.

199

Charm

魅

清平乐

村居

辛弃疾

茅檐低小
溪上青青草
醉里吴音相媚好
白发谁家翁媪

大儿锄豆溪东
中儿正织鸡笼
最喜小儿无赖
溪头卧剥莲蓬

Clear and Peaceful Music: Life in the Village

Xin Qiji (1140–1207 CE)

Eaves on their thatched hut low and neat,
　　green grass on the nearby stream.
Quite drunk, they flirt in a southern drawl,
　　this old affectionate pair.

Their oldest hoes beans to the east of the brook,
　　the second weaves chicken-coop reeds—
Whilst the youngest, mischievous, loveable imp,
　　peels lotus, sprawled on the bank.

201

Charm

魅

静夜思

李白

床前明月光
疑是地上霜
举头望明月
低头思故乡

Thoughts on a Still Night

Li Bai (701–762 CE)

So bright the gleam by the foot of this bed —

    has frost already arrived?

I lift my head and gaze at the moon —

    look down and think of old home.

203

Charm 魅

长恨歌

白居易

汉皇重色思倾国
御宇多年求不得
杨家有女初长成
养在深闺人未识
天生丽质难自弃
一朝选在君王侧
回眸一笑百媚生
六宫粉黛无颜色
春寒赐浴华清池
温泉水滑洗凝脂
侍儿扶起娇无力
始是新承恩泽时
云鬓花颜金步摇
芙蓉帐暖度春宵

The Song of Unending Regret

Bai Juyi (772–846 CE)

The Great Tang Emperor, presiding over all,

    craved a beauty to topple an empire.

Seeking never finding, till at last

    he saw a daughter of the Yang, a girl not fully grown.

Raised deep within the courtyard, quite unknown,

    her heavenly beauty was impossible to ignore;

With a single backward glance, she charmed him a
hundredfold—

    the painted darlings of the Six Palaces paled beside her.

In early Spring, she bathed in the Flower Clear Pool,

    whose soothing waters smoothed the flawless perfection

    of her skin.

So tender and delicate, as maids helped her from the
fountain,

    at once, the Emperor fell, bestowing his grace on her.

With her cloud-like hair and flower face, her golden pearly
 hairpins,

    they spent their nights behind hibiscus screens.

Charm

魅

春宵苦短日高起
从此君王不早朝
承欢侍宴无闲暇
春从春游夜专夜
后宫佳丽三千人
三千宠爱在一身
金屋妆成娇侍夜
玉楼宴罢醉和春
姊妹弟兄皆列土
可怜光彩生门户
遂令天下父母心
不重生男重生女
骊宫高处入青云
仙乐风飘处处闻
缓歌慢舞凝丝竹
尽日君王看不足
渔阳鼙鼓动地来
惊破霓裳羽衣曲

But in short Spring nights, the sun soon rises,

    and the Emperor missed dawn audiences.

He indulged her—revelry, banquets without cease—

    she rode with him in daytime, but the nights were solely

    hers;

Three thousand beauties languished at court,

    but he lavished three thousand affections on her body

    alone.

She'd flirt in the Golden Room, attending him all night,

    after Jade Tower banquets, they'd doze together tipsy.

Her brothers and sisters were granted court titles,

    she brought honour to her family and clan.

Gradually the hearts of parents across the Empire

    changed to favour girls not boys.

The Black Horse Palace could almost touch the clouds,

    but her divine music drifted on the wind for all to hear.

Her slow song, her unhurried dance, with strings and flute,

    the Emperor gazed at her unceasing throughout the

    day—when suddenly—

War drums from Yuyang rolled out, shaking the earth,

    shattering her dance of Rainbow Skirt and Feather Tunic.

Charm

魅

九重城阙烟尘生

千乘万骑西南行

翠华摇摇行复止

西出都门百余里

六军不发无奈何

宛转蛾眉马前死

花钿委地无人收

翠翘金雀玉搔头

君王掩面救不得

回看血泪相和流

黄埃散漫风萧索

云栈萦纡登剑阁

峨嵋山下少人行

旌旗无光日色薄

蜀江水碧蜀山青

圣主朝朝暮暮情

行宫见月伤心色

夜雨闻铃肠断声

Smoke and dust poured from the watchtowers on the nine
layered gates;
The Emperor's army, with a thousand chariots, ten thousand
horses
    fled towards the south-west, but stopped after a hundred
    miles;
Six battalions would march no further—
    they would crush the moth-eyed beauty of the Yang
    to death under their horse's hooves, before another step;
Hairpins of gold and jade fell to the ground yet no one picked
them up.   209

The emperor could not save her; with covered face,
    he turned to look, blood and tears streaked across his
    cheek.
Yellow dust filled the wind as it wailed and sighed—
    as they took the twisted pathway to Sword Pavilion.
In the shade of Mount Omei, where few ventured,
    the Emperor's banners paled in the thin sunshine;
Midst smoky mountains and limpid streams,
    the Emperor lay lovelorn from dawn to dusk.

He looked at the moon with a grief-filled heart;
    in the night rain, a bell tolled, tearing at his guts.

Charm

魅

天旋地转回龙驭
到此踌躇不能去
马嵬坡下泥土中
不见玉颜空死处
君臣相顾尽沾衣
东望都门信马归
归来池苑皆依旧
太液芙蓉未央柳
芙蓉如面柳如眉
对此如何不泪垂
春风桃李花开日
秋雨梧桐叶落时
西宫南内多秋草
落叶满阶红不扫
梨园弟子白发新
椒房阿监青娥老
夕殿萤飞思悄然
孤灯挑尽未成眠
迟迟钟鼓初长夜
耿耿星河欲曙天

Heavens whirled, the earth turned—he sought his chariot,
  steps hesitant, rooted to the spot;
there, at Tall Horse Slope, under soil and dirt,
  lay his lustrous white beauty, lost to all.
Ruler and lords wept on their sleeves at this grief,
  whilst eastwards towards the city gates, the horses brought
  them home.

The pools and gardens were just as he'd left them—
  in Taiye Lake lotus flowered, willows still swayed in the wind;
He saw her face in every petal, her eyebrows
  in each thin branch—his tears would never cease.
Spring winds blew down the blossoms of peach and plum,
  autumn rain pulled leaves from the phoenix tree;
The West and Southern Palaces stood choked with autumn
grass,
  red leaves on the terraces lay in heaps unswept.

In the Pear Garden, her courtiers' hair now grey,
  handmaidens in the Pepper Tree Court already old.
Fireflies dart in the twilight as he broods alone without end,
  the lamp wick burned right down, yet still he cannot sleep.
Bell and drum toll the night hours as they drag
  and stars shine out in the dawn's first light.

Charm

魅

鸳鸯瓦冷霜华重
翡翠衾寒谁与共
悠悠生死别经年
魂魄不曾来入梦
临邛道士鸿都客
能以精诚致魂魄
为感君王辗转思
遂教方士殷勤觅
排空驭气奔如电
升天入地求之遍
上穷碧落下黄泉
两处茫茫皆不见
忽闻海上有仙山
山在虚无缥缈间
楼阁玲珑五云起
其中绰约多仙子
中有一人字太真
雪肤花貌参差是
金阙西厢叩玉扃
转教小玉报双成
闻道汉家天子使

The frost lay thick on the glazed roof tiles—
 his kingfisher quilt cold as stone; no lover to share it now.
Slowly the years part life from death,
 her soul never once left his dreams.

To court, there came a Taoist monk from Linqiong,
 known for reaching spirits by magic arts;
The court, to lighten the Emperor's mood,
 beseeched the shaman to seek out her ghost.
He floated on space, riding the air, darting like lightning,
 searching through heaven and earth to the underworld.
Failing everywhere to find whom he sought
 till he heard the spirits tell of an isle above the sea.
Formless, ethereal, floating in haunted mists,
 honeycombed towers rose through five coloured clouds.
Holding transcendental beings, all benign—
 including the one called "Great Truth"—
Whose snow-white skin and flower-like face were hers.

In hope, he knocked at the jasper door,
 in the watchtower on the western palace wall;
His message passed one hand maiden to the next,
 to tell of the waiting envoy.

Charm

魅

九华帐里梦魂惊
揽衣推枕起徘徊
珠箔银屏迤逦开
云鬓半偏新睡觉
花冠不整下堂来
风吹仙袂飘飘举
犹似霓裳羽衣舞
玉容寂寞泪阑干
梨花一枝春带雨
含情凝睇谢君王
一别音容两渺茫
昭阳殿里恩爱绝
蓬莱宫中日月长
回头下望人寰处
不见长安见尘雾
惟将旧物表深情
钿合金钗寄将去
钗留一股合一扇
钗擘黄金合分钿
但令心似金钿坚
天上人间会相见

She started from her dream under the nine-flower canopy;

    pushing aside pillows, she grabbed her clothes.

Threw open the pearly screen and silver gate,

    her billowing hair fell to one side.

Embroidered hat set carelessly, she ran,

    wind fluttering through sleeves,

      as if she danced with Rainbow Skirt and Feather Tunic;

Her silent, jade-like face criss-crossed with tears

    like raindrops on a pear branch in Spring.

With steady gaze that showed her feelings,

    she bade the Emperor's envoy, tell him that since they'd

    parted his voice and form were strange to her:

In the Bright Sun Hall, love and grace were absent—

    the days and months were long in this ghostly place;

She turned to look on the realm of men,

    sight blurred by clouds of dust and fog.

Charm

魅

Moved by the monk's words, she found her old love tokens—

    a box inlaid with shell, a hairpin of burnished gold.

From the shell box, she broke away one side to keep

    from the hairpin, she split one fork;

临别殷勤重寄词
词中有誓两心知
七月七日长生殿
夜半无人私语时
在天愿作比翼鸟
在地愿为连理枝
天长地久有时尽
此恨绵绵无绝期

She bade the envoy take them to her lover,

　　with the deepest, closest secret,

Known only to their beating hearts.

　　"Council your heart to be as firm as shell and gold.

　　On that seventh day in the seventh month, in the Palace

　　of Long Life,

　　we vowed to each other privately at night.

　　Some day in heaven or earth we'll meet again;

　　in heaven, we'll be two birds with a single set of wings,

　　on earth, we'll be two trees with trunks entwined."

217

Heaven is long and Earth is old,

　　and both may end someday—

Whilst this undying regret

　　will last for ever and ever.

Charm

魅

赠卫八处士

杜甫

人生不相见
动如参与商
今夕复何夕
共此灯烛光
少壮能几时
鬓发各已苍
访旧半为鬼
惊呼热中肠
焉知二十载
重上君子堂
昔别君未婚
儿女忽成行
怡然敬父执
问我来何方
问答乃未已
儿女罗酒浆
夜雨剪春韭
新炊间黄粱

For Wei, My Secluded Friend Who Seeks No Office

Du Fu (712–770 CE)

Two paths in life might never intertwine,

    like morning and evening stars.

Tonight then is a rare event—

    Together—you and I—in the candlelight.

We were young and lusty not so long ago,

    now grown grey at the temples.

We inquire of old friends, find half are ghosts—

    that shocks us and turns in our guts like grief.

How could we have known it'd be twenty long years,

    'til I'd visit your home once again?

When I left, you were single,

    now, these boys and girls in a row—

Congenially honour their father's old friend,

    enquire from whence I have travelled.

We talk for a while and then,

    they serve your finest wine—

With spring chives cut in the night rain,

    a bowl of freshly cooked sorghum.

219

Charm

魅

主称会面难
一举累十觞
十觞亦不醉
感子故意长
明日隔山岳
世事两茫茫

Poems

诗
歌

220

My host complains it's so hard to meet
   and urges me to take a tenth cup.
But who cares about ten cups of drunkenness,
   when old feelings remain here unchanged?
Tomorrow the mountains will separate us—
   our cares borne away by the wind.

Charm

魅

梦李白二首（其一）

杜甫

死别已吞声
生别常恻恻
江南瘴疠地
逐客无消息
故人入我梦
明我长相忆
恐非平生魂
路远不可测
魂来枫林青
魂返关塞黑
君今在罗网
何以有羽翼
落月满屋梁
犹疑照颜色
水深波浪阔
无使蛟龙得

Dreaming of Li Bai

Du Fu (712–770 CE)

Separation by death?—in the end you get used to it,

    separation in life?—that's continuing grief.

Fever rises to the south of the River,

    no word from you, Old Friend?

You've been in my dreams,

    as if you know how I miss you.

It seems you're no long mortal,

    so great the distance between us.

Your spirit flies over gum-tree woods,

    and returns over dark mountain forts.

Old Friend, you're trapped in nets and snares—

    can you find the wings to fly free?

The moonlight falls on my cottage roof

    perhaps it is shining on you?

The waters between us are deep and wide,

    don't let the River Gods take you.

223

Charm

魅

访戴天山道士不遇

李白

犬吠水声中
桃花带露浓
树深时见鹿
溪午不闻钟
野竹分青霭
飞泉挂碧峰
无人知所去
愁倚两三松

Visiting the Taoist Priest at Mount Daitian but Not Finding Him

Li Bai (701–762 CE)

A dog's bark drifts through the waters sound,

    dew hangs thick on peach tree flowers.

The trees grow deep, a deer at times appears,

    but no bell can be heard at the midday stream.

Wild bamboo divides the mist at dusk,

    a spring hangs airborne against a distant peak.

Yet no one knows where the old monk's gone,

    so I rest on a pine or two.

225

Charm

魅

宿业师山房，期丁大不至

孟浩然

夕阳度西岭
群壑倏已暝
松月生夜凉
风泉满清听
樵人归欲尽
烟鸟栖初定
之子期宿来
孤琴候萝径

Waiting at the Teacher's Mountain Lodge for Ding, Who Has Not Arrived

Meng Haoran (689–740 CE)

The sun sinks low on Western Ridge,
  gulleys fill quickly with shade.
Pines in the silvery moonlight,
  cool in the gathering dusk.

Sounds of wind and water,
  ring out full and clear.
Woodsmen head home weary,
  birds alight, then are still.

And you, I expect,
  will stay here a while?
So I—alone with my zither—
  will wait on the bindweed path.

227

Charm 魅

夜归

杜甫

夜半归来冲虎过
山黑家中已眠卧
傍见北斗向江低
仰看明星当空大
庭前把烛嗔两炬
峡口惊猿闻一个
白头老罢舞复歌
杖藜不睡谁能那

Returning Late at Night

Du Fu (712–770 CE)

As night draws in, I return on Tiger Road,
    the mountains grow dark—at home all sleep.
The Great Bear descends towards the river,
    overhead, the stars vast as space.

Before the house stand candles—two glaring flames—
    in the ravine, a monkey shrieks.
Tho' white-haired and old, I chant my songs—
    with pigwood staff, I do not sleep
    and all is safe and sound.

229

Charm

魅

留别妻

苏武

结发为夫妻
恩爱两不疑
欢娱在今夕
嬿婉及良时
征夫怀往路
起视夜何其
参辰皆已没
去去从此辞
行役在战场
相见未有期
握手一长叹
泪为生别滋
努力爱春华
莫忘欢乐时
生当复来归
死当长相思

Departing Words for His Wife

Su Wu (c140–60 BCE)

Since our hair was plaited as man and wife,
    neither has doubted our love.
Let us celebrate tonight,
    and enjoy good times while they last.

Remembering where I must travel;
    I spring up and stare at the sky.
Orion and Scorpio grow dim in the East —
    I must leave with a short lament.

I am going on service, away to war,
    our reunion date unknown.
I hold your hand with a restless sigh;
    tears flow as our lives pare apart.

Enjoy the springtime with all your strength
    and think of the days we were happy.
If I live, I will come back —
    if I die, remember me always.

231

Charm 魅

【 美 | Beauty 】

noun: the quality present in a thing or person that gives
intense pleasure or deep satisfaction to the mind,
whether arising from sensory manifestations, a
meaningful design or pattern or a personality or place
through which high spiritual qualities are manifest
adj (beautiful) : wonderful, very pleasing or satisfying

Here the poets draw on nature for inspiration. Chinese thought is suffused with a sense that all human attempts to dominate the universe are self-defeating and that, far from trying to dominate non-human nature, man's aim should be to live in harmony with it. The poets display a heightened sense of pleasure and tranquillity from living at peace with the natural world rather than being its adversary. 'I cannot recount the endless beauty here,' writes Li Qingzhao as she watches waves crest on a lake. Elsewhere, Bai Juyi takes money to buy flowering trees: 'I simply bought whatever had blooms, not caring if peach or plum. A hundred fruits, all mixed together; a thousand branches, flowering in due rotation.' Others lament the hacking down of forests— 'Great rafters of cypress, in such a disaster, just for the fires in the armoury?' asks Liu Zongyuan in the ninth century. Others bemoan the poaching of predators, such as the hawk: 'Now caged, with drooping feathers...in the wilderness, rats and raccoons were just pests, at night now ten times they startle and attack.'

在这里，诗人们从大自然中获得灵感。中国人的思想中深深萦绕着一种感知，即人类所有主宰宇宙的企图总会弄巧成拙，人类的目标应该是与自然和谐相处，而不是试图主宰人性之外的大自然。诗人们通过与自然世界和平相处，而非与之为敌，展现出了一种高度的愉悦和宁静。李清照一边看着湖面上的涟漪，一边写道："说不尽，无穷好。"白居易花钱买开花的树："但购有花者，不限桃杏梅。百果参杂种，千枝次第开"。也有人哀叹森林被大肆砍伐，比如柳宗元曾在九世纪时写道："柏梁天灾武库火？"还有人抱怨偷猎捕食性动物，比如偷猎猎鹰："羽翼脱落自摧藏，草中狸鼠足为患，一夕十顾惊且伤"。

读山海经十三首（其一）

陶渊明

孟夏草木长

绕屋树扶疏

众鸟欣有托

吾亦爱吾庐

既耕亦已种

时还读我书

穷巷隔深辙

颇回故人车

欢言酌春酒

摘我园中蔬

微雨从东来

好风与之俱

泛览周王传

流观山海图

俯仰终宇宙

不乐复何如

Reading the Book of Hills and Sea

Tao Yuanming (c365–427 CE)

In the first month of summer, plants already tall,
    all around my cottage, the trees are leafy and neat.
The birds seem glad wherever they alight,
    and I — I love my little hut.
My seeds are fully planted,
    at times, I read my books.
The lanes outside so furrowed,
    old friends turn back in their carts.
With spirits high, I pour Spring wine,
    take greens from the courtyard plot.
The faintest rain blows in from the East,
    and brings a wholesome wind.
I read vaguely of ancient kings,
    eyes roving across the *Book of Hills and Sea*.
In a single glance I see the whole cosmos —
    how could I not be content with all this?

Beauty

美

晚晴

杜甫

返照斜初彻
浮云薄未归
江虹明远饮
峡雨落余飞
凫雁终高去
熊罴觉自肥
秋分客尚在
竹露夕微微

Clear Evening

Du Fu (712–770 CE)

Last rays slant clear on the skyline,
Torn clouds blown far away.
A rainbow falls to the river,
    as raindrops swirl in the gorge.

Wild ducks soar in the heights,
Brown bears feed fat on the banks.
In autumn, strangers still linger
    at dew on the evening bamboo.

239

Beauty 美

戏答元珍

欧阳修

春风疑不到天涯
二月山城未见花
残雪压枝犹有橘
冻雷惊笋欲抽芽
夜闻归雁生乡思
病入新年感物华
曾是洛阳花下客
野芳虽晚不须嗟

A Playful Answer to Yuanzhen

Ouyang Xiu (1007–1072 CE)

The spring wind doubts it can reach me,

    here at the ends of the earth.

In March this year,

    no flowers grace city or hill.

Fierce snow bends the branches,

    yet tangerines still cling on.

Cold thunder startles bamboo,

    as shoots sprout soft from the ground.

The sound of returning geese at night,

    bring thoughts of my old hometown.

Whilst bedbound over New Year,

    I yearned for nature's splendours.

Once as a guest in Luoyang,

    I stayed under flowering trees.

Blossoms are late this year,

    but I'll wait and not despair.

Beauty

美

东坡种花二首（选一）

白居易

持钱买花树
城东坡上栽
但购有花者
不限桃杏梅
百果参杂种
千枝次第开
天时有早晚
地力无高低
红者霞艳艳
白者雪皑皑
游蜂遂不去
好鸟亦栖来
前有长流水
下有小平台
时拂台上石
一举风前杯
花枝荫我头
花蕊落我怀
独酌复独咏
不觉月平西

Planting Flowers on the Eastern Embankment

Bai Juyi (772–846 CE)

I took money to buy flowering trees,

    planting them out to the east.

I simply bought whatever had blooms,

    not caring if peach or plum.

A hundred fruits, all mixed together,

    a thousand branches, flowering in due rotation.

Each has its season, early or late,

    to all alike the fertile soil is kind.

Red ones hang like a heavy mist,

    white ones gleam like the snow.

Wandering bees cannot bear to leave them,

    fine birds come here to roost.

In front flows an endless stream,

    below, the terrace is flat.

At times I sweep its flagstones,

    at others, I raise my cup.

Branches shade my weary head,

    whilst buds drop down on my lap.

Alone I toast my fortune—alone I chant my verse—

    unaware of the moon in the west.

243

Beauty

美

巴俗不爱花

竟春无人来

唯此醉太守

尽日不能回

These Sichuan folk care not for flowers,

in Springtime nobody came.

But I their drunken Governor,

will stay here long after dusk.

Beauty 美

田舍

杜甫

田舍清江曲
柴门古道旁
草深迷市井
地僻懒衣裳
榉柳枝枝弱
枇杷树树香
鸬鹚西日照
晒翅满鱼梁

Rustic Hut

Du Fu (712–770 CE)

My rustic hut in a clear river's bend,
    the wicket gate close by the road.
Tall reeds shade me from the bustling lanes,
    as I loaf in my tattered smock.

A willow branch sways
    through the medlar tree scent—
Whilst drying their wings in the sun's last rays,
    the cormorants crowd on the pier.

247

Beauty 美

怨王孙

李清照

湖上风来波浩渺
秋已暮　红稀香少
水光山色与人亲
说不尽　无穷好
莲子已成荷叶老
清露洗蘋花汀草
眠沙鸥鹭不回头
似也恨　人归早

On the Lake the Wind Blows Waves Far into the Distance

Li Qingzhao (1084–c1151 CE)

Wind rises across the lake,

    waves spread boundless and crest in the air.

Autumn's almost over, red leaves sparse,

    scent long gone.

Light shines upon the water whilst mountain colours

    move the hearts of men.

I cannot recount the endless beauty here —

In lotus pods, seeds are fully ripe,

    the lily leaves all grown old.

Clear dew glistens on the clover,

    that spreads on the grassy banks.

Gulls and herons do not deign

    to raise their heads,

Regretting the return of men.

Beauty　美

新城道中二首

苏轼

东风知我欲山行
吹断檐间积雨声
岭上晴云披絮帽
树头初日挂铜钲
野桃含笑竹篱短
溪柳自摇沙水清
西崦人家应最乐
煮葵烧笋饷春耕

身世悠悠我此行
溪边委辔听溪声
散材畏见搜林斧
疲马思闻卷旆钲
细雨足时茶户喜
乱山深处长官清
人间歧路知多少
试向桑田问耦耕

The New City Road

Su Shi (1037–1101 CE)

The east wind knows I long to walk in the hills,

    but blows the rain round my eaves.

Clouds drape the slopes like silken caps,

    treetops hang 'neath the coppery gong.

Wild peach blossoms smile, my bamboo fence too short,

    willows wave, the brook runs clear.

Simple mountain folk—the happiest of men—

    boil mallow, fry bamboo, prepare the soil for Spring.

The path of life is like this leisurely tour,

    my horse wanders as I loosen his reins by the stream.

Factions struggle at court but ordinary folk just look on

    like logs that fear the searching axes.

My worn out war horse longs for the battle's end,

    whilst tea farmers delight in the ample rain.

In this quiet mountain place, tucked away from chaos,

    there are still some honest scribes.

How much can one know at this crossroads in life?

    —try the mulberry groves and ask the plowmen there.

Beauty　美

行路难三首（其二）

柳宗元

虞衡斤斧罗千山
工命采斫代与椽
深林土剪十取一
百牛连鞅摧双辕
万围千寻妨道路
东西蹶倒山火焚
遗余豪末不见保
蹢跦涧壑何当存
群材未成质已夭
突兀峥嵘空岩峦

The Road is Hard to Pass

Liu Zongyuan (773–819 CE)

Axes and hatchets spread across a thousand hills;
    at the Works Commissioner's decree:
"Hack down all trees for posts and rafters."

Deep in the woods the workmen toil
    but only a tenth of the trunks are hauled away
    before—catastrophe!

A hundred harnessed oxen break their shafts:
    Great trunks and towering logs topple,
    block the paths and roads both east and west,
    whilst hilltops blaze with fire.

Beauty 美

Even the smallest twigs are trampled
    left to rot amongst the chaff.
No tree is left in gulley or ravine;
In sudden bareness, valleys lie empty
    the cliffs and peaks shorn clean.

柏梁天灾武库火

匠石狼顾相愁冤

君不见南山栋梁益稀少

爱材养育谁复论

"Great rafters of cypress, in such a disaster,
    just for the fires in the armoury?"
Woodsmen look back like wolves,
    to survey this sad injustice.
Can they still see the roof-tree
    of the far-off Southern Mount?
Source of nurture and nourishment,
    ripped from this beloved place,
All should reflect on all this.

Beauty

美

笼鹰词

柳宗元

凄风淅沥飞严霜
苍鹰上击翻曙光
云披雾裂虹霓断
霹雳掣电捎平冈
砉然劲翮剪荆棘
下攫狐兔腾苍茫
爪毛吻血百鸟逝
独立四顾时激昂
炎风溽暑忽然至
羽翼脱落自摧藏
草中狸鼠足为患
一夕十顾惊且伤
但愿清商复为假
拔去万累云间翔

Lines on a Hawk in a Bamboo Basket

Liu Zongyuan (773–819 CE)

Chill wind noisily sifts the hard frost,
    as a goshawk whirls in the dawn.
Clouds shatter, mists crack, a rainbow snaps in half.

Like lightning, the hawk skims a hilltop
    his wings cut through bushes and thorns.

Snatching foxes and hares, he mounts the sky once more,
    hair on claw, blood on beak, a hundred birds all gone.
Alone he stands—eager, proud—and surveys his dominion
below
    but fiery wind, damp heat rush on,
    now caged, with drooping feathers,
    his tired wings ache with pain.

In the wilderness, rats and raccoons were just pests,
    at night ten times they startle and attack.
If only he could harness the gathering autumn wind,
    and break free from these shackles,
    he would soar once more, up through a thousand clouds.

Beauty 美

【 真 ⏐ Truth 】

adj (true) : legitimate, rightful

noun: faithful conveyance of that which is recognisable

from life experience, conformity with fact or reality, verity

adj (true) : real, genuine, authentic, firm in allegiance,

loyal, faithful, steadfast, unfailing, virtuous

Truth examines the universal realities of life; that each of us is allotted a finite span; that we exist as individuals only within wider society; that we all face the same fate. Chinese thought has been shaped by war and strife, so the balance between individual rights and collective responsibility is different from our own. 'Men should value the welfare of all above the happiness of one,' writes Bai Juyi as he lies wrapped in a warm coat thinking of those outside in winter. Elsewhere after tax collectors arrive at his house, he is relieved of the guilt of knowing he had not paid his fair share; 'today, at last, my heart is at ease, as I pay the tithes from my barn.' We find a charcoal seller, freezing but hoping for a cold snap; 'The clothes on his back ... so wretched—his coat so thin! Yet, anxious his fuel might lose value, he longs for icy weather.' And Wang Anshi, the great Song Chancellor, asks 'What man would fight for a hairbreadth's gain?' The poets also show wistful sadness at the passing of youth and the greatest of them all, Du Fu, finally laments, 'Have my poems not given me a name in this world, tho' I retired as I should, now I'm old? Floating, floating, like what?—I don't know—my whole life just bird tracks on sand.'

"真"审视生活的普遍现实：我们每个人生命有限，我们作为个体只存在于更广泛的社会中，我们也都面临同样的命运。中国人的思想受到战争与冲突的影响，个人权利与集体责任的平衡点与我们不同。白居易裹着温暖的大外套，想着外面那些在冬日里受冻的人，写道："丈夫贵兼济，岂独善一身。"在另一首诗中，因为收税人到他家中，他终于可以不再为没有纳足税而感到内疚，"今日谅甘心，还他太仓谷"。我们还看见白居易笔下的卖炭翁，自己冻得瑟瑟发抖，却盼着天再冷一点，"可怜身上衣正单，心忧炭贱愿天寒"。宋朝了不起的丞相王安石也曾问道："君子忍与争秋毫？"诗人们也对青春易逝感到悲伤，最伟大的诗人杜甫最终深深感叹："名岂文章著，官应老病休。飘飘何所似，天地一沙鸥。"

春望

杜甫

国破山河在
城春草木深
感时花溅泪
恨别鸟惊心

烽火连三月
家书抵万金
白头搔更短
浑欲不胜簪

Gazing Out Over Spring

Du Fu (712–770 CE)

The state lies shattered—

    yet the hills and rivers survive,

The city walls this spring—

    are deep with trees and grass.

These times it feels like flowers—

    are splashed with bitter tears,

I jolt from my lonely sorrow—

    at the cry of a distant bird.

263

The beacons have been lit—

    ablaze for three months now,

I'd give ten thousand pieces—

    for a letter from faraway home.

I scratch my head and feel—

    my hair is stretched so thin,

The wisps of white can't hold—

    my commissioner's hatpin down.

Truth 真

城南上原陈翁，以卖花为业，得钱悉供酒资；又不能独饮，逢人辄强与共醉。辛亥九月十二日，偶过其门，访之，败屋一间，妻子饥寒，而此翁已大醉矣。殆隐者也。为赋一诗

陆游

君不见

会稽城南卖花翁

以花为粮如蜜蜂

朝卖一株紫

暮卖一枝红

屋破见青天

盎中米常空

卖花得钱送酒家

取酒尽时还卖花

春春花开岂有极

日日我醉终无涯

Old Chen (Who Sits by the Southern Wall and Sells Flowers for Money to Buy Drink) Did Not Like to Drink Alone and Asked Anyone to Join Him. Poem on Chancing on the Family, 12th September, 1191, Calling on Their Broken One-room Shack, Wife and Children Hungry and Cold, the Old Man Already Blind Drunk, Now Almost a Recluse.

Lu You (1125–1210 CE)

Have you not seen the flower man at Southern Gate,

    the one who scoffs flowers like a bee?

At dawn, he'll sell us a bud of purple,

    at dusk it's a sprig of red.

His roof so broken the clear sky looks right through

    and his rice barrel is generally empty.

When he gets money from flowers,

    he makes for the inn.

When it's all spent,

    then he just sells more flowers.

Right through the springtime,

    the flowers bloom continuously.

And each day he is drunk beyond limit.

Truth 真

亦不知天子殿前宣白麻
亦不知相公门前筑堤沙
客来与语不能答
但见醉发覆面垂鬖鬖

What does he care of the Emperor's proclamations,

or if the dykes by the gates are just sand?

When customers greet him, he can't even reply,

his locks hang down on his comatose face.

267

Truth 真

卖炭翁

白居易

卖炭翁

伐薪烧炭南山中

满面尘灰烟火色

两鬓苍苍十指黑

卖炭得钱何所营

身上衣裳口中食

可怜身上衣正单

心忧炭贱愿天寒

夜来城外一尺雪

晓驾炭车辗冰辙

牛困人饥日已高

市南门外泥中歇

翩翩两骑来是谁

黄衣使者白衫儿

手把文书口称敕

The Old Man Who Sells Charcoal

Bai Juyi (772–846 CE)

The old man who sells charcoal—

    cuts firewood, burns it up on Southern Hill.

Grimed with ash, face streaked with smoke from the fire,

    his grey hair grizzled, each finger inky black.

What living can he make from this miserable fuel?

The clothes on his back

    the food in his mouth.

So wretched—his coat so thin!

Yet, anxious his fuel might lose value,

    he longs for icy weather.

That night, snow fell deep round the city walls,

    at dawn his cart rolled on icy ruts.

His ox distraught, half starved before the sun grows high,

    they rest in slush by the Southern Gate.

Who are these two who come trotting up so effortlessly?

Court messengers, in yellow coats and vests of white,

    clutching edicts, barking orders,

269

Truth 真

回车叱牛牵向北
一车炭　千余斤
宫使驱将惜不得
半匹红纱一丈绫
系向牛头充炭直

Poems 诗歌

270

They turn the cart and, with curses, haul it north,

with its charcoal load, more than

a thousand pounds in weight.

They whip the ox ahead—what can the old man do?

"Half a bolt of red gauze and a single roll of damask,

trussed up on your ox's head,

more than enough for your meagre winter fuel!"

271

Truth

真

新制布裘

白居易

桂布白似雪
吴绵软于云
布重绵且厚
为裘有余温
朝拥坐至暮
夜覆眠达晨
谁知严冬月
支体暖如春
中夕忽有念
抚裘起逡巡
丈夫贵兼济
岂独善一身
安得万里裘
盖裹周四垠
稳暖皆如我
天下无寒人

Poems 诗 歌

My New Padded Gown

Bai Juyi (772–846 CE)

White as snow the Guilin cloth,

    soft as clouds the Suzhou silk;

Thick with wadding,

    my gown grows sumptuously warm.

Wrapped in its folds I sit from dawn till dusk;

    covered with it at night I sleep till day,

Who could remember the harsh moon of Winter,

    with their body as warm as the Spring?

Midnight—a sudden thought seized me,

    I pat my gown and rise to pace the room.

Men should value the welfare of all

    above the happiness of one.

If only a ten thousand mile gown

    enfolded the Earth's four corners,

All would be as warm as I—

    with no one cold outside.

273

Truth 真

新花

王安石

老年少忻豫
况复病在床
汲水置新花
取慰此流芳
流芳秖须臾
我亦岂久长
新花与故吾
已矣两可忘

Newly Cut Flowers

Wang Anshi (1021–1086 CE)

It's not much fun in later years,

    stuck in bed and sick.

I pour some water, arrange the flowers,

    eased by their drifting scents.

Scents adrift yet rooted for that fleeting moment,

    I wonder how long I can last.

Fresh cut flowers and my long-lost self,

    both so soon forgotten.

Truth 真

纳粟

白居易

有吏夜叩门
高声催纳粟
家人不待晓
场上张灯烛
扬簸净如珠
一车三十斛
犹忧纳不中
鞭责及僮仆
昔余谬从事
内愧才不足
连授四命官
坐尸十年禄
常闻古人语
损益周必复
今日谅甘心
还他太仓谷

Poems 诗歌

Paying Taxes in Millet

Bai Juyi (772–846 CE)

At night they came, officers at my door,

    banging, shouting for my dues in millet.

No one dared to wait for dawn,

    lanterns and candles on the great barn floor.

Passed through sieves, grain clean as pearls,

    heaped on a cart, thirty bushels in all.

Doubting my tax is fully paid,

    with whip and lash, they scold my servant boys.

277

Long ago, I gained official rank,

    tho' I knew I lacked the talent.

Sat like a dead man through four long posts,

    collecting ten years worth of tithes.

Oft I hear from ancient times,

    loss and gain come round in their turn.

Today, at last, my heart is at ease,

    as I pay the tithes from my barn.

Truth 真

洗儿戏作

苏轼

人皆养子望聪明
我被聪明误一生
惟愿孩儿愚且鲁
无灾无难到公卿

Playful Words on Bathing My Baby Boy

Su Shi (1037–1101 CE)

When raising a child

    parents want cleverness.

I, through intelligence,

    walked into error.

I hope that this child will be

    oafish and dim.

Then without suffering—without much effort—

    he'll rise to Cabinet rank.

279

Truth 真

秋思

陆游

利欲驱人万火牛
江湖浪迹一沙鸥
日长似岁闲方觉
事大如山醉亦休
衣杵相望深巷月
井桐摇落故园秋
欲舒老眼无高处
安得元龙百尺楼

Thoughts of Autumn

Lu You (1125–1210 CE)

The desire to win is irresistible—like an army of oxen,

    crashing forth with flaming brands on their horns—

Yet I am as carefree as a wandering gull.

Days grow long and become a year,

    but I am too lazy to notice,

Matters weighty as mountains disperse in my cup of wine.

By the river, they beat clothes in readiness for winter;

    moonlight falls deep in the lanes.

Leaves float down from the phoenix tree,

    autumn comes to my withered yard.

Is nowhere high enough to rest my dim eyes—

    where is my hundred foot tower?

Truth

真

村夜

陆游

寂寂山村夜
悠然醉倚门
月昏天有晕
风软水无痕
迹为遭谗远
身由不仕尊
敢嗟车马绝
同社自鸡豚

Evening in the Village

Lu You (1125–1210 CE)

Evening grows silent in Mountain Village,
    pensive, I lean at my door.
The moon shines dim in the twilight haze,
    the pond undisturbed by the breeze.

Slander drove me from my official post,
    now idle, I've recovered my worth.
How could I sigh at losing my carriage,
    when here I raise chickens and pigs?

283

Truth 真

感悟妄缘，题如上人壁

白居易

自从为骍童
直至作衰翁
所好随年异
为忙终日同
弄沙成佛塔
锵玉谒王宫
彼此皆儿戏
须臾即色空
有营非了义
无著是真宗
兼恐勤修道
犹应在妄中

Awakening to the Random Nature of Fate: Written on the Wall of a Monk's Cell

Bai Juyi (772–846 CE)

Since I was a senseless youth

    'til now I'm old and grey,

My passions shift with the changing years.

    but I yearned to be busy 'til the end.

Conjuring pagodas from a handful of sand,

    clanking stone ornaments at Court.

But these thoughts are simply trifles,

    in the end, all craving is gone.

The self can't be found through working,

    the unwritten might lead us to truth.

Devotion alone can't redeem us—

    just accept chaos in life.

285

Truth 真

买花

白居易

帝城春欲暮

喧喧车马度

共道牡丹时

相随买花去

贵贱无常价

酬直看花数

灼灼百朵红

戋戋五束素

上张幄幕庇

旁织巴篱护

水洒复泥封

移来色如故

家家习为俗

人人迷不悟

有一田舍翁

偶来买花处

低头独长叹

此叹无人谕

一丛深色花

十户中人赋

Buying Flowers

Bai Juyi (772–846 CE)

Spring nears its end in the capital,
Carts and horses clomp in the lanes.
At this, the time of peonies,
Folks gather round market stalls.
"Cheap or pricey, there's no standard here
Depends on the number of blooms.
Flowers ablaze—the finest reds:
Smaller buds—like rolls of silk. "
Awnings shelter the flowers,
With fences plaited like screens.
"Spray them with water, seal roots back in mud,
Move them about, they'll not lose their hue."
Everyone follows this custom,
Enthralled by the brilliant blooms.

An old man from the fields
   came by chance that way.
Head bowed with a drawn-out sigh—
   a sigh no one could explain.
"One bundle of these deep red buds,
   ten households' tax would pay."

287

Truth

真

狂言示诸侄

白居易

世欺不识字
我忝攻文笔
世欺不得官
我忝居班秩
人老多病苦
我今幸无疾
人老多忧累
我今婚嫁毕
心安不移转
身泰无牵率
所以十年来
形神闲且逸
况当垂老岁
所要无多物
一裘暖过冬
一饭饱终日
勿言舍宅小
不过寝一室

Crazy Words for All of My Nephews

Bai Juyi (772–846 CE)

The world cheats those who cannot read—

    I, unworthily, am practiced in literature.

The world cheats those who hold no office—

    I, unworthily, was blessed with high rank.

As years go by, there are aches and pains—

    I, luckily, feel none of those ills.

As years go by, there is trouble and bother—

    Now I'm done with family and kids.

My heart is at peace, not distracted

    my body is calm, not exerted.

For ten years now,

    my spirit is free, unconstrained.

Approaching twilight years

    there's no need of material things.

One gown to pass warm through the winter.

One meal to get through the day.

Don't say my house is too tiny!

I only need one room to sleep.

Truth 真

何用鞍马多
不能骑两匹
如我优幸身
人中十有七
如我知足心
人中百无一
傍观愚亦见
当己贤多失
不敢论他人
狂言示诸侄

What use for a team of horses,

When I can't ride more than just one?

As fortunate as I?

　—perhaps seven in ten.

As contented as I?

　—not one in a hundred.

In other's affairs, even fools are wise.

But the wise can err in their own.

I don't dare to debate this with others—

These mad words are just for my nephews.

291

Truth 真

收盐

王安石

州家飞符来比栉
海中收盐今复密
穷囚破屋正嗟欷
吏兵操舟去复出
海中诸岛古不毛
岛夷为生今独劳
不煎海水饿死耳
谁肯坐守无亡逃
尔来贼盗往往有
劫杀贾客沉其艘
一民之生重天下
君子忍与争秋毫

Confiscating Salt

Wang Anshi (1021–1086 CE)

Around the shoreline, warrants fly dense as comb's teeth,

    along the coast, salt confiscation grows stricter than ever.

Poverty moans and sobs under broken rooves,

    the starving creep out once the inspectors move on.

This scattering of islands, lean and barren from ancient times,

    where islanders struggle for life.

If they don't boil sea water, they starve and that's the end
of it,

    who can be an official and be unmoved by all this?

The destitute forced into banditry —

    they rob and kill the traders, scuttle all their boats.

The life of one civilian weighs as heavy as the Empire —

    what man would fight for a hairbreadth's gain?

Truth

真

别岁

苏轼

故人适千里
临别尚迟迟
人行犹可复
岁行那可追
问岁安所之
远在天一涯
已逐东流水
赴海归无时
东邻酒初熟
西舍豕亦肥
且为一日欢
慰此穷年悲
勿嗟旧岁别
行与新岁辞
去去勿回顾
还君老与衰

Leaving at the End of the Year

Su Shi (1037–1101 CE)

When a friend starts out on a journey of a thousand miles,

    as he is about to leave, he delays again and again.

A journey of miles may be retraced,

    but the journey of years can never be rerun.

As for that year, where has it gone?

    far beyond the ends of the earth—

Gone like a river that flows to the East,

    flushed into the ocean with no hope of return.

My neighbours to the east have begun to heat wine,

    in the house to the west, they've fattened a boar.

They'll soon have their one day of joy,

    to soothe a whole year's trouble.

Let's not regret the passing of a year,

    we'll soon bid farewell to the next.

Everything passes, no one ever looks back

    as we grow old and weak.

295

Truth 真

僧庐

陆游

僧庐土木涂金碧
四出征求如羽檄
富商豪吏多厚积
宜其弃金如瓦砾
贫民妻子半菽食
一饥转作沟中瘠
赋敛鞭笞县庭赤
持以与僧亦不惜
古者养民如养儿
劝相农事忧其饥
露台百金止不为
尚愧七月周公诗
流俗纷纷岂知此
熟视创残谓当尔
杰屋大像无时止
安得疲民免饥死

Poems 诗歌

The Monks' Home

Lu You (1125–1210 CE)

The beams in the monastery daubed with emerald
and gold,
  petitions fly like an urgent call to arms.
Well-healed merchants sit on hefty piles
  and throw away gold like broken tiles.

Folks in the fields have beans to eat,
  but one failed crop and they'll be starving in a ditch.
Whipped with thorns for taxes, red splatters the debtors yard,
  Yet—for monks—they still give more.

The ancients cared for farmers like their own,
  urged them forward, feared famine might return.
Benevolent emperors didn't waste money on dew terrace
gardens,
  they'd be shamed by poets of their times.
But these clowns—they don't get any of that,
  accustomed to seeing the wounded—the broken—
  so long as it's not of their own.

Without an end to great halls and statues,
  can folk evade hunger and death?

297

Truth

真

读史

王安石

自古功名亦苦辛
行藏终欲付何人
当时黮黯犹承误
末俗纷纭更乱真
糟粕所传非粹美
丹青难写是精神
区区岂尽高贤意
独守千秋纸上尘

Reading History

Wang Anshi (1021–1086 CE)

Hasn't making a name always been a bitter and toilsome task?
Who can be trusted with the in's and out's of the story?
Even at the time it was murky and baffling—
Gossipers tangle the threads, mix the truth with their lies.

Passing down dregs, essence left behind,
Histories can't grasp the spirit of the times.
How can their sketchy lines convey the meaning of a sage?
Alone, the reader turns pages, with dust of a thousand years.

Truth

真

除夜直都厅，囚系皆满，日暮不得返舍，因题一诗于壁

苏轼

除日当早归
官事乃见留
执笔对之泣
哀此系中囚
小人营糇粮
堕网不知羞
我亦恋薄禄
因循失归休
不须论贤愚
均是为食谋
谁能暂纵遣
闵默愧前修

Dusk at New Year's Eve in the Prefectural Court with Prisoners and Not Releasing Them

Su Shi (1037–1101 CE)

It's New Year's Eve, and I really should be home,

    yet the office keeps me here long beyond its time.

I take up my brush and find myself tearful,

    pitying the poor prisoners who stand before my court.

Just ordinary people scrambling for food—a few crumbs—

    caught in a net, with no idea of shame.

But I myself—don't I love my meagre salary?

    My toeing-of-the-line spoils my only chance of peace.

No need here to debate who's worthy or witless,

    Everyone's just angling for a meal in the end.

Could I free them for a while at least, I wonder?

    In shame, I fret silently before the ancients who did.

301

Truth

真

轻肥

白居易

意气骄满路
鞍马光照尘
借问何为者
人称是内臣
朱绂皆大夫
紫绶或将军
夸赴军中宴
走马去如云
樽罍溢九酝
水陆罗八珍
果擘洞庭橘
脍切天池鳞
食饱心自若
酒酣气益振
是岁江南旱
衢州人食人

Light (Furs) and Fat (Horses)

Bai Juyi (772–846 CE)

On bright saddles that light up the dust,
Arrogance fills up the road.
If asked what is known of these riders
Men say, "They've cabinet posts."
Red seal-cords denote the high ministers
Great generals have medals of mauve;
Decked up for an officer's banquet,
On horses that float like the clouds.

303

Goblets and pitchers brim with mellow wine,
Delicacies from land and water grace their table.
Splitting tangerines with their thumbs,
Slicing scaled fish from Heavenly Lake.

Truth

真

After eating, they feel so content,
Their smugness puffs up with the wine—
This year there is drought on the Yangtse,
In Quzhou, men eat their own kind.

旅夜书怀

杜甫

细草微风岸
危樯独夜舟
星垂平野阔
月涌大江流
名岂文章著
官应老病休
飘飘何所似
天地一沙鸥

Record of Feelings from a Night of Travel

Du Fu (712–770 CE)

The faintest wind bends the shoreline grass,

    my jutting mast soars lone in the night.

Stars hang high across the boundless wilds,

    moonlight streams and the great river flows.

Have my poems not given me a name in this world,

    tho' I retired as I should, now I'm old?

Floating, floating, like what?—I don't know—

    my whole life just bird tracks on sand.

305

Truth 真

Translation of Introduction

前言译文

一　缘起与感谢

　　那一年，雨下个不停。雨水从秋天开始倾泻，顽强地一直下到冬天。连续几周，大雨仿佛带着某种坚定的意志倾盆而下，以至于我担心自己的房子恐怕都要被淹了。

　　我刚搬来不久，对周围的环境还不熟悉。在现在这种气候变化的年代，朋友们曾劝我不要在河岸边买房子，但我却爱上了那个石顶小屋和附近那座建于十二世纪的破旧的修道院。我注意到有一群鸭子从我的窗前游过，穿过那个最近被我当成花圃的地方，于是我在家门口垒起一排沙袋，严阵以待。最后，河水不过是在门阶上溅起一些水花就退却了。我深感幸运。听说威尔士有个村庄，那里每天都在下雨，已经下了八十四天了。真不知道怎么会有人受得了。我觉得自己身上潮乎乎的，正是过节的时候，我却没来得及安排活动，便赶紧给朋友们寄去贺卡，顺带放了一首中国诗人苏轼在一千年前写的诗，这首诗似乎既适合这个季节，也与我的新住处十分相宜。

今年又苦雨，两月秋萧瑟。
卧闻海棠花，泥污燕脂雪。

春江欲入户，雨势来不已。

小屋如渔舟，蒙蒙水云里。
空庖煮寒菜，破灶烧湿苇。
那知是寒食，但见乌衔纸。

　　朋友们对这些诗句的反应和兴趣让我感到十分惊讶，所以在接下来的几个月里，随着冬去春来，我开始寻找描写明媚春光的诗句。我越深入研究中国诗歌就越被这些古诗的当代相关性所震撼。尽管时空不同，但我们每天的新闻头条都像是从这些书页里跳出来的。

　　中国最伟大的诗人之一是一个战争难民，他在一千二百年前进行写作。从读到他的第一首诗起，我脑海中就浮现出一个饱经风霜忧心忡忡的形象，他站在城墙上，望着被洗劫一空的城市和被战争蹂躏的土地，急切地盼望听到家人的消息。我进一步探寻，发现很多诗人都关注社会不公的现象，比如无家可归、财富分配不均、逃税，甚至还有食物赈济。在其他诗中，还有关于年老受辱的诗句，比如秃顶、掉牙，有的则描述了临终前的困苦。也有诗人提到了对自然资源的无限制开发对环境造成的破坏，例如过度砍伐森林，以及消灭捕食者对食物链造成的影响。读到这些诗，让人感觉就好像盖亚理论已经回响了十个世纪。还有诗人为幼子的夭折而悲伤，或为社会的流动性而烦恼。我甚至从八世纪诗人的自发性中看到了物质滥用和双相型障碍的影子，因为他们常常喝得酩酊大醉，然后突然蹦起来，随手抓起一支毛笔，在墙壁上、屋顶上、地板上、家具上大笔一挥写出一幅难以辨认的狂草。这听起来倒像是中世纪的狂欢。然后我读到了公元1079年的"乌台诗案"，一位诗人为言论自由大力辩护却遭到

流放。渐渐地，我勾勒出了唐宋时期诗人的轮廓，并开始翻译他们的文字，下面就是我的发现。

中国诗歌是巨大的文明资产。它是所有时代所有文化中规模最大的连贯文学，它涵盖了成千上万——可能是数十万首诗，从公元前二十三世纪到现在，中间从未间断。中国诗歌和英国诗歌确实不同，但二者在思想和感情上有重叠。中国诗歌的情感是普世的，但表达方式却是独一无二的。诗歌在中国社会中占据着中心地位，中国人一直十分享受引用诗歌的乐趣。很多代人以来，诗歌对中国人有很多方面的影响，比如想象力、野心、欲望和希望，比中国的其他文化分支的影响都要深远。诗歌浓缩了中国人内心深处的信念和感受，塑造了中国这个伟大古老文明的现代表现形式。这种决定性的文化灵性深深融入了所有中国人的 DNA 中。欣赏中国诗歌背后的思想可以找到一扇通向当代中国思想的窗户。

在本书中，我选择了能够表达中国人日常生活情感的诗歌，而不是试图编纂一部中国古代诗歌选集。如同我的前人一样，我惊叹这些诗句跨越千年的光辉，想让它们有更广泛的受众，让中国诗歌有一天能被视为整个人类共同的财富，而不是像在西方那样只被几个专家研究。但对那些更务实的人而言，我也有另一个动机。随着中国在不断变化的世界秩序中重返舞台中央，中国已经开始影响中国以外数百万人的生活。对于那些想在未来保持话语权的人来说，理解中国人的思维模式无疑是十分有益的。我想说明了解这些诗歌如何能给在国内外与中国打交道的外国人提供直接的操作层面的帮助。

虽然我都是从原文直接开始翻译的，但翻译遇到困难的

时候，我总能从前人的译作中得到指引。很多学者已经创作了许多精彩而鼓舞人心的译本，例如托尼·巴恩斯通、周平、戴维·欣顿、林培瑞、宇文所安、比尔·波特、王红公以及已故的伟大先驱阿瑟·韦利等。我向他们所有人致敬，我很荣幸能够坐在这些大师们脚边。

我要感谢金奇先生将我引入中国诗歌之门，感谢卡丽·格蕾西帮忙审读初稿，感谢麦乔和麦启安坚持让我写这本书，还有他们提供的源源不断的杜松子酒，感谢欧嘉明、尼古拉斯·巴伯、安思文和姜斐德精彩的评论，让我能够有更广阔的视野，感谢欣然为我构建中国诗歌的宏大图景并为我解释那些疑难部分。我还想感谢杜克雷愿意把她珍贵的中国诗集藏本借给我，我一度以为我把那些书弄丢了，而她却并不十分担心。我还要感谢尼奇·汉瑟对本书源源不断的兴趣、支持和善意。我想感谢我的好朋友和同事李剑锋，这么多年来，他不厌其烦地为我解释中国文化和历史，面面俱到，这笔人情债，我算是背着了。我还想对我才华横溢而谦逊的译者徐懿春表达由衷的欣赏和钦佩，她的辛勤工作让我的英文创作更加顺畅。我还要感谢商务印书馆的马浩岚、郭朝凤和我的编辑杜茂莉，她是一个特别认真的编辑。最后，我衷心感谢詹妮·劳伦斯，她不懈的鼓励对我这个作者而言意义重大。

本书第一版将由中国商务印书馆出版，所以本书第一批读者是中国人。如果一位中国作家写了一本关于莎士比亚的书，我们可能不会为了加深对莎翁作品的理解而去读这样一本书，但我们可能会为了了解这位中国作家走过的路以及他或她遇到的困难而去读这本书。我们可能会忍受命运的暴虐的毒箭，或者可能会挺身反抗人世无涯的苦难，也可能跟一

群"趿着拖鞋的龙钟老叟"笑谈人生的七个阶段。但最重要的是,到最后当一切尘埃落定,我们会后退一步,携手并肩,默默惊叹于莎士比亚揭示的人生的普遍真理。中国的诗人们也和莎士比亚一样。

祈立天
2021,惊蛰

Translation of Introduction 前言译文

$$\sigma_x \sigma_p \geq \frac{\hbar}{2}$$

海森堡的不确定性原理

二 海森堡的不确定性原理

中国人对于不确定性的随意总是让我震惊。西方人与中国人不同，怎么说呢，西方人对不确定性总有一些难以名状的不安。西方人总是必须确切地知道将会发生什么，总是寻求解释而不愿坦然接受，亦总是渴望每一个故事都有明明白白的结局。至少三百年来，西方科学一直在试图精确地阐释我们所处的世界。然而讽刺的是，这种追求对世界的完美解读终结在了海森堡手中。1927年，海森堡提出了著名的"不确定性原理"，为现代物理学奠定了基础，变革了科学思维方式。与此同时，他的这一理论也给可知的事物设置了绝对的限制。爱因斯坦完全不赞同这一理论，曾经怒斥道："上帝才不会掷骰子。"

在我看来，上帝根本就不玩骰子，他老人家可太忙了。然而看看上一页上那个简短的不等式，不得不承认海森堡改变了现实世界的意义。波变成粒子，粒子又变成波，宇宙就这样坍缩成一系列概率分布。长期以来，人们不断探索和追寻完美的世界，成功制作出了元素周期表，用牛顿力学完美地描述了行星运行的轨道——实际上或许并不完美，然后又用微积分让众多行星在各自的轨道上和谐地运行，但最终这些探索与追寻却被不确定性原理逼入绝境。当海森堡将不确

定性编织到时空架构中，西方关于可知论的假设动摇了，但与此同时，他所提出的理论对中国人来说却很容易接受，因为早在几千年前，中国人就把这样的不确定性一针一线地编织进了自己的语言。

三 中文的不确定性

海森堡论文原稿的标题[1]中有一个词很难确切地翻译成英文，我倒真心希望他是故意这么写的。据专业人士所言，anschaulichen 是德语中无法明确翻译的一个词。

海森堡选的这个词被翻译成"实体的""可感知的"或是"知觉的"。我依稀记得曾在某处读到，最贴近 anschaulichen 的字面翻译大概是"可见的"，然而没有人能够说出哪一个词最贴切，我就安心了。当一门语言转换成另外一种的时候，本就常常会出现歧义，好比说从德语到英语。如果源语言本身就有一些模糊，而不仅仅是两种语言的转换之间模棱两可，那就很容易营造出万花筒般迷幻而又混沌的世界。

在中文里，不精确已经成为了日常生活的一部分。世界各地的律师、计量人员和精算师会被这种不精确气得冒烟，中国人却已经习以为常。日常用语和思维方式中的模糊不清，让人们易于接受日常观察所得而不求甚解。例如对于中医，虽然它不能用科学来解释，但正如我的一个朋友曾经不无讽刺地说："中医让你糊里糊涂地活，西医让你明明白白地死。"

与德语或是匈牙利语相比，中文的语法基本上是不存在

1　"Ueber den anschaulichen Inhalt der quantentheoretischen Kinematik und Mechanik"

的。比如在描述不同时间段的动作时，动词保持不变：

今天早饭，我吃（了）泡菜。

昨天早饭，我吃（了）泡菜。

明天早饭，我（要）吃泡菜。

我们的语言中早已消失的东西在中文里仍然存在，像下面这两句话：

成吉思汗（曾）是个很不错的家伙。

和

成吉思汗是个很不错的家伙。

这两句话在中文里无法区分。"曾经是"以及"现在是"在语言上和逻辑上并没有什么分别，仿佛中国的过去与现在融合在了一起。

中文的名词和代词并不体现性[1]数格。"一本书、两本书、三本书、四本书"，"她给他三本书"或"她给她三本书"，还有"他给他三本书"，根本搞不清楚是怎么回事。到最后你可能还在纳闷难道是这三本书把他给了她。

中文里也没有冠词和不定冠词。传统意义上来说，中文没有标点符号，也没有主格、宾格、与格、所有格或离格来为难冥思苦想的孩子们，只有一系列让人头昏脑涨的概念和超大的词汇量。据我所知，中文里至少有五万三千个汉字。[2]

中文中大量的同音字增加了口语的不确定性。这些字发音完全相同或极其相似，叫人头脑发胀，舌头打结。我的口袋字典里有超过 50 个字的发音都是 shi，选取几个作为示例：狮、虱、柿、蓍、铈（化学元素）、屎、尸、诗、轼（古代车

---

1 Ta 可以表示"他""她"或者"它"，我承认这几个字写法不同。

2 来源于《中华大辞典》。

厢前用作扶手的横木）。难怪字典的书页都被磨薄了，都是人们拼命翻出来的。当然了，我知道你们会说，说中文的人可以通过四个不同的声调来区分这些似乎完全一样的字，但我还是想要强调这一点，比如说有二十几个不同的字的发音都是 shū，发一声，但是它们的意思却包括：书本、梳子、叔叔、菽（豆类）、蔬菜、疋（脚）、𦈡（粗麻布）、枢（门上的转轴），以及殳（古代的一种竹制兵器）。[1]

因此，当一个字脱离语境或没有语境时，人们不得不费九牛二虎之力才能猜出这个字来。比如说，跟中国人握手的时候，常能听到他们这样说："你好，我是本部门的科长，姓张，弓长张。"或者是："我是副市长，我姓汪，汪洋的汪，不是大王的王。"所以我认为，在这一点上不论你怎么分辩，如果一个字没有解释，没有清晰的语境，那么单凭发音很难或者几乎不可能确定到底是哪个字。

有一次，我的一位朋友在餐厅里点了一杯凉开水，但是女服务员听完却一脸为难。中文里没有时态之分，我大概能猜到她是在想我朋友指的是滚烫的沸水还是烧开过的水。于是我朋友进一步解释道："要一杯凉的开水。"这下更糟糕了，服务员看起来一脸茫然，我似乎都能看出她的脑子里在想到底什么是凉的开水。我朋友顿了一下，然后完整的解释了一遍：

"麻烦给我一杯原本是冷水然后煮开了又放凉的水，这样我才能确保它是干净的。"

"好的，"服务员回答道，表情一点儿也没变。

但是其实这里面还有一个更复杂的问题。我朋友说的是

1　中文普通话口语有四个声调，即（i）pāi，一声，（ii）pái，二声，（iii）pǎi，三声，（iv）pài，四声。

"凉的开水"，意思是"冷却的沸水"，但听起来几乎跟"两个开水"发音一模一样，而后者的意思是"两杯开水"，所以我们又经历了一个来回才解决了所有的问题，终于可以喘口气了。[1]

还有一次，我的朋友在酒店里打电话给前台说被子脏了，结果过几分钟门口来了一位服务员，带着一托盘干净的杯子。bèizi（四声）的意思是被子，而 bēizi（一声）的意思是水杯。yán 指的是盐，而 yān 指的是香烟。类似的例子不胜枚举。tiānxià 指的是全中国，也可以指全世界，看你用在什么地方了。tuǒxié 的意思是妥协，但 tuōxié 指的是拖鞋。我无聊的时候喜欢想象一些来访的商人在合同谈判中敲打桌子并疯狂地大喊："我们做了数不清的拖鞋，现在该你们做一些了。"我怀疑中国人听到这个会狠狠翻个白眼。最后，ǎo 意为善良的老太太，千万不要跟 áo 混淆，因为后者指的是传说中的一只巨大的乌龟。[2]

书面语也同样让人困惑。打个比方，"己""已""巳"是三个完全不同的字，意思分别是"自己（jǐ）""已（yǐ）经"和地支的第六位"巳（sì）"，光解释清楚这个就可以写一篇短文了。"李""季""孝"三个字也没好到哪儿去，[3] 更别说"休"字和"体"字了。蜜蜂在英文中是 bee，但是如果你把这两个字的顺序调换一下，就变成了蜂蜜（honey）。我是

1 很抱歉，我曾在别处讲过这件轶事，但是我必须承认，我实在想不出更贴切的例子。

2 更加让人震惊的是"鲚"和"痔"的发音都是 zhì（四声），却分别指沙丁鱼和痔疮。

3 如你所料，它们的意思分别是"李子""季节"和"孝顺"。

铁定分不清哪个是哪个的。

　　在书面语中，还有一个概念叫做"偏旁"，它能够与其他模糊的语音元素构成完整的字。这些偏旁许多本身不具有实际意义，但是能体现由其构成的汉字的整体属性。例如，氵（三点水旁）通过三点水来暗示水的元素，因此，有湖、江、港、滩。扌（提手旁）表示手或抓，犭（反犬旁）表示狗或动物，而宀（宝盖头）表示屋顶。然而这些偏旁并不能孤立出现，只有与其他汉字元素组合起来才有意义，才能组成完整的汉字。

　　因此，"平"这个字本身的意思是平衡的、平坦的或平静的，在与其他偏旁组合的时候会构成意义不同的汉字。你不觉得"平"这个字本身看起来带着一种平衡感和镇定感吗？"平"与鱼相结合，就成了"鲆"，意思是扁鱼，如比目鱼；与土结合，就成了"坪"，意思是平坦的台地；跟木组合，则变成"枰"，意思是扁平的木器具，如棋盘或木制床。到目前为止，这一切似乎都在合理范围内。当"平"与三点水旁（氵）和草字头（艹）组合的时候，则变成"萍"，意思是浮在露天池塘表面的浮萍。与口组合，变成"呯"，指迅速爆炸的声音或者呯的一声。但是可以想象，这种明显的秩序很快就会被打破，例如像"肨"（意思是多脂肪的或油性的[1]）和"蚲"（意思是蚯蚓），这两个字都没法与平坦联系起来，特别是蚲字，除非是被人踩过的蚯蚓。因此，人们虽然常常可以根据偏旁来猜字意，根据发音元素来猜读音，例如以上列举

1　这个字表示腹胀的意思时念 pēng，像这样的多音字的存在让学这门语言的学生苦不堪言，肨这个字能立刻让你想起这种痛苦。

的各种 píng 字，但这种方式从来都不够可靠。

更糟糕的是同一个字可能会有多种意思，有些意思可能还相互矛盾。例如"恨"这个字有讨厌和后悔的意思，你不觉得这两个意思完全不一样吗？"苍"这个字在一部字典里的解释是青蓝色、青绿色、青黑色或银白色；[1]而"须臾"一词既指极短的时间又有从容的意思，这两个意思在我看来是对立的。"抚"可以意味着爱抚，也有扇耳光的意思，我觉得这两个动作似乎完全不同。[2]一个字所包含的意思可以如此之丰富，以至于很难确定该用哪一种。曾经有一个项目[3]试图编纂一本综合汉英词典，然而第一次印刷后发现，光定义"子"这个字就耗费了六十八个双栏页面，更别说其他很多字根本没有任何含义，只是为了押韵或用于表示令人费解的修饰关系，该项目随即在 1955 年便被舍弃了。

有时候中文也有精确性，但还是会让人疑惑不解，这是因为那些汉字的精确程度使得他们几乎不可能被使用。例如，有一个字专指在地里从北向南拉车，另外还有一个完全不同的字专指从东往西拉车。"咢"的意思是击鼓而不作歌。还有"箕裘（jīqiú）"在某本词典中被定义为"制作筛子和皮衣的工艺"。[4]筛子和皮衣，这不禁让人喃喃自语，这二者又是从何而来呢？再说一个，"轼"[5]这个字在某处被定义为

1　"苍"的意思在我看来指的是远处云雾缭绕的青山的朦胧色彩，但这也很难说，因为和"黄"搭配以后它的意思似乎还有困惑和倒置或翻转。

2　这两个动作真的不一样吗？比如 stroke 这个单词，six strokes 的意思是打六下（用鞭子），he stroked the cat 的意思是他抚摸猫（通常不用鞭子）。

3　哈佛—燕京学堂项目。

4　www.chinese-dictionary.org

5　这个字与著名诗人苏轼的名字是同一个字。

"乘坐马车或战车时用半弓敬礼（伏轼致敬）"。最后，我还曾遇到过一个字，是用来描述"远看仿佛一大群虫子的某种东西"。[1]当我后来发现这个字源于一部号称《天朝仁学广览》的杜撰作品时，我感到非常恼火，事实上它压根儿不是一个字。不过这些至少证明了我并不是唯一一个对这些令人匪夷所思的中文辞藻感兴趣的人，我也如同其他人一样，深陷在中文这片迷雾中。

除了单个字的含义之外，中国人对于那些让人完全摸不着头脑的含糊语句似乎也处之泰然。或许那些说不出来、讲不清楚、听不明白的东西正是复杂生活的某种庇护，能给人们带来些许平静，这谁又能说得明白呢？[2]

恕我冒昧地举个例子，我曾经和一位中国商业伙伴就一个工厂的监管问题发生了冲突，好几个人因此进了医院。事情是这样的，我们花了三年的时间试图安排一位财务总监来管理我们的资金，然而，在经历了多次挫败之后，我们偶然发现了一起重大欺诈行为，于是爆发了冲突。在冲突期间，我听说市委书记，也就是本市的一把手正在当地一家酒店吃饭，于是我来到他和同事用餐的房间外等他。令我没想到的是，他同意见见我。

跟他会面的时候，我采用了中国同事建议的委婉做法，

Translation of Introduction　前言译文

1　这个字属于一个虚构的生物分类，其中包括：(i) 皇帝的 (ii) 不朽的 (iii) 被驯化的 (iv) 乳猪 (v) 美人鱼 (vi) 难以置信的 (vii) 流浪狗 (viii) 形容疯癫而颤抖的 (ix) 用骆驼毛刷描绘的。

2　有一次我问一个中国朋友本书中第 200 页辛弃疾的诗歌中第七句提到的"最喜小儿"是指"最疼爱的小男孩"还是"最开心的小男孩"，朋友问我为什么觉得这很重要，因为最开心的小男孩很可能就是最受宠的那个。

避免直来直往地说。在描述欺诈行为时，我说的是："资产管理确实有问题。"他面不改色地回答道："事出有因。"若是有人敢把这番对话的意思直译出来，那么我说的"资产管理确实有问题"这句话的实际含义是："那些混蛋刚从我们那里偷走了 800 万镑，而你们这些当官的压根儿撒手不管！"而他的回答"事出有因"这句话，更准确的翻译应该是："你们蠢到把所有的钱投进去还不派一个会计来看着，你们还指望什么呢?！"

四 来自八世纪的回响

　　中文的不精确，如前所述，会让世界各地的会计和理赔员火冒三丈，然而如果我们超越日常用语而谈及诗歌，便会发现正是这份不精确给读者提供了空间。

　　中国诗歌没有动词而有动态，没有形容词而有形，没有代词而有指代。虽然可以说所有的艺术，尤其是诗歌和文学，在某种程度上都是一种"翻译"，因为它是通过一面棱镜来解读的，这面棱镜里折射的是读者的个人经历、预期和渴望，然而中国诗歌中的模糊性使得想象力能够发散到意想不到的广阔维度。"花非花，雾非雾"，即"像花而不是花，似雾而不是雾"，这句诗是一千多年前，由中国最伟大的诗人之一以一种罕见的坦率写下来的。[1] 这短短六个字，就像曾有人若有所思地说的那样："谁能透过记忆的幕布，看清原石最本真的模样？"[2]

　　因此，当谈到翻译中国诗歌时，一个雄心勃勃而缺乏经验的新手，比如我，肯定会不自量力地在下面这七个嶙峋怪异且难以撼动的巨石上碰壁。

　　<u>无主语</u>：在中国古典诗歌中省略主语乃是常态。就像在

1　真的坦率吗？我怀疑白居易其实是在描写情人的阴道。

2　《城市的画像》中亚当·威廉姆斯曾这样说。

现代的短信中一样，读者必须自行推断动作的发出者。"邮件看到了"，是被谁看到了？虽然这种语义上的模糊对于我们所有人来说都习以为常，走在路上随手发条短信或是因为着急赶车而简单写几句，在这样的语境下含义确实是显而易见的，然而走入诗歌微妙的意境中后，复杂程度则会呈指数级增长。

有一首著名的五言绝句，首句是这样的："空山不见人"，没有谁会觉得这句诗里"空山"才是主语，只因为它是一个名词且位于句首。根据常识推断，这句诗的主语应当是诗句中未曾提及的一个人。但是，怎么样才能用必须明确主语的西方语言表达出这种效果呢？如果在诗句中插入"我"，那么整句诗便会带入诗人的想法而破坏掉那种无他而自在的意境。

<u>无数量</u>：如前所述，中文的名词不体现数量。"A rose is a rose is a roses.（玫瑰指一朵玫瑰，也指一束玫瑰。）"实际上这指的当然不只是一朵玫瑰花（或者也不是一束），而是指玫瑰这种事物本身。就像 tableness 这个单词一样，想必你也赞同这种说法，tableness 不是指单张桌子的数量汇成的总和，比如一场你完全不想参加的婚礼上的桌子，而是指桌子这种东西的特质，你觉得呢？可是这个你让翻译怎么翻，翻成"桌性"听起来怪怪的，而翻成"桌态"就是胡扯，但是这就是中国人想要表达的意思。

<u>无时态</u>：中文有多种方法来表明某件事是已经发生、将要发生还是正在你眼皮子底下发生，但是这些方法不包括动词时态。对于诗人而言，正是时态的缺失营造出了一种朦胧的美感。我未曾在山上看到人吗？还是此刻我看不到任何人？抑或是我想象着看不见人会是什么感觉？或者是他、她，

或是他们看不到人？所有这些都有可能，还有其他可能性。由于时间模糊，根本分不清太阳在同一个地方到底是升起来了还是落下去了。这些诗的真正含义就像是在量子力学概率空间中不知不觉飞舞的微小粒子，我们知道它们在那里，但永远不能真正看清它们，也不可能直接观察而确定它们到底在哪里。

引经据典：与文艺复兴时期的绘画一样，中国诗歌常常隐含典故。例如对当权者的批判往往蒙着面纱，要是没有几个"中国古典习语"的博士学位，普通人往往读不出来。一首诗看似在歌颂皇家狩猎的威严，实际上可能是用对束手就擒的弱小动物的屠杀来类比暴君对普通百姓的压迫。但是，对于暴君的影射往往只是用历史文学事件或人物性格的寥寥数语带过，因为如果诗人讲得明明白白，那么恐怕他和他的家人就要马上被砍头了。

特定的花卉和动物常常象征某种品质，例如，菊花代表着恒久和长寿，因为秋天百花凋零，只有菊花不畏秋霜，傲然开放；莲花代表纯洁，因为其出淤泥而不染；鸳鸯象征着夫妻之间的忠贞，因为它们交颈缠绵终生；大雁的直线高飞象征着对目标坚定不移，而其 V 字形雁阵象征着对等级制度的尊重，有时大雁的迁徙还象征着离家千里的旅人。这样的象征不胜枚举。柳树代表浮躁、轻浮，甚至是沦落风尘，因为它们在风中折腰；松树则象征长寿和正直坚守原则，因为松树并不因季节变换而变色；竹子也深受学者喜爱，因为寒冬凛冽，绿竹仍不改其颜色，风霜雨打，绿竹亦不折其腰；梅花象征刚毅，因为它在严寒中开百花之先，独天下而春；梧桐树，有时也被称为凤凰树，象征着感情丰沛，因其木质洁

白柔软，宜制乐器，可以表达奏乐者的万千情愁。[1]

简洁：上面提到的中文的模糊与简洁是相结合的，或者更准确地说是信息密度大，这一点可要让其他地方的小报作家羡慕不已了。有一个故事是这么说的，大约一千年前，一位大诗人与同僚们在翰林院[2]外等待的时候，目睹了一件不同寻常的事，一匹受惊的马在繁华的街道上横冲乱撞，踩死了睡在街上的一条狗。诗人问他的两位同僚该怎么以书面形式描述这一事件，一人写道："有犬卧于通衢，逸马蹄而杀之。"另一人写道："有马逸于街衢，卧犬遭之而毙。"诗人笑说，"按你们这般修史，怕是一万卷都写不完啊。"那二人问诗人该怎么说，诗人淡定地回答道："逸马杀犬于道。"但如果把中国的诗歌像小报标题似的逐行翻译会毁了那些诗的，真不知道该怎么翻译。

韵律：虽然诗歌的意义呈现出模糊性和刻意的灵活性，但另一方面，诗歌的结构可能非常死板。中文里的大多数诗歌每一行都严格地限定为五个或七个汉字。稍后你便会看到，由于这种规律，这些诗歌多以长方形呈现在书页中。这种结构使得诗歌按照某种韵律展开，而又因为每行诗歌压缩的信息量巨大，在翻译成英文的过程中，很难充分捕捉到所有的意思。

排列：如果一个字有两种意思，那么虽然困难但还能忍

1　据我所知，在西方世界也有类似的象征，例如，在古希腊的诗歌中，石榴代表着旺盛的生殖能力，因为石榴有很多种子。

2　翰林的意思是文翰之林，翰林院是一个精英的学术与管理委员会，设立于公元八世纪，其职能是梳理和诠释经典，以及为后文提到的科举考试确定规则。

受。如果一行诗中的五个字各有两种意思，那么整行诗的所有意思的排列总和，按照数学家们的算法，则是 2 的 5 次方。那么对于译者而言，就是有 32 种意思。

如果每个字有三种意思，最后会出现 243 种排列。如果每行中的汉字数从五个变为七个，那么相对应会出现 2187 种排列。但是很多字都有五六种意思，没什么好说的，我还是举个例子吧。

在本书第 192 页《长干行》一诗中，王红公把第 17 句"五月不可触"翻成："你不应该冒着五月洪流的风险"，而巴恩斯通和周平把这一句翻作："我与你，已有五个月没有接触了"。

这些译者每个人都为数百首诗提供了精彩而准确的见解，这些见解没有对错之分，让人深受启发。然而在我们被数不清的数学排列组合杀得片甲不留的时候，便不得不作出自己的选择。[1] 事实上，华兹生，一位了不起的中国和日本诗歌的翻译家曾这样评论中国最伟大的诗人之一："在翻译杜甫的诗作时有很多不同的方法来解决相关的翻译问题，这也是为什么我们需要尽可能多的翻译版本。"

23

---

1 我自己的版本是："到如今我已有五个月没办法感受你"，因为我没法假装看不到这首诗中的渴望，而且我也想要保持它的韵律。

五　夸克和色禁闭

　　朋友们，在与中国诗歌建筑的短暂邂逅之后，想必你们已经领略到它不时展现出的惊人的结构不稳定性。那么现在，我们即将来到这本书最困难的部分，还望各位多多包涵。

　　当我们进入到亚原子粒子的世界中时，如果你对此深感绝望绝对情有可原，但是拜托还是先别绝望。如果在这部分你碰到许多生僻词，请忽略它们，继续往下看，现在我也不太理解这些词了。事实上，量子物理学的先驱之一，曾被爱因斯坦本人提名诺贝尔奖的沃尔夫冈·泡利，曾经就令人眼花缭乱的亚原子粒子的数量说道："早知道有这么多，我就去学植物学了。"所以你们不是一个人在战斗，我也保证不会在这里停留太久。

　　让我们从古希腊人开始吧。早在公元前六世纪，古希腊人就认为物质是众多微小粒子的集合。快进二十五个世纪来到公元 1805 年，我们看到一个可怜的织布工，他穷得付不起儿子的学费。这个孩子叫约翰·道尔顿，住在曼彻斯特。我们看到他在湖区的山峰上踱步，先是捣鼓着气象测量，后来又开始关注原子。沿着古希腊人的脉络，他发现每一个元素都是由不同的"原子"或"ἄτομος"组成，"ἄτομος"的意思是"不可分的东西"。

然后是门捷列夫，他在西伯利亚的一个小村庄中挣扎着脱贫，梦想着圣彼得堡洋葱头教堂圆顶上镀金的十字架。1869年，门捷列夫将道尔顿的所有元素都编到一张元素周期表中，不仅为混沌的自然带来秩序，还预测了几个当时尚未被发现的元素。或许更重要的是，他还负责将俄罗斯伏特加酒的酒精含量标准定为百分之四十，要是我的话怎么着也得定成百分之五十。

既然已经分出了原子，那么化学家们便可以开始构建分子了。但是，假如我们没有追随化学家的步伐进入到那个充斥着塑料、尼龙和肥料的更大的世界（谁能够抵制这个世界呢？），而是跟随粒子物理学家走入亚原子的世界一探究竟，你觉得我们会在原子里面发现什么呢？

1896年，一个在剑桥工作的新西兰人发现原子可能能被分成更小的带电荷的部分，电子由此被发现。十年之后，卢瑟福因为某些原因用阿尔法粒子撞击薄金片，发现原子里大部分空间是空的，但在中心有一个极小的原子核，其四周则被电子所环绕。不久后，卢瑟福又撞击了两个氮原子，随即发现原子核含有质子。我觉得卢瑟福这个人大概是很喜欢撞东西吧。

最终在1937年，一个来自北方的棉纺工人的儿子发现了中子。所以三位先驱科学家，汤普森、卢瑟福和查德威克，共同创造了物质的原子模型，他们都曾在剑桥的卡文迪什实验室工作。他们的天才之处是提出原子本身包含一个由质子和中子构成的带正电的原子核，电子以某种方式在轨道中围绕原子核旋转。

故事接下来的走向该是远距离观察太空了，或者更确切

地说，我们必须观察从遥远的星系流向太阳系的高能粒子流，或叫"宇宙线"。天体物理学家尚不确定这些宇宙线的来源，但有一个叫做"大熊"或大熊座的星座可能是超高能射线的来源。这些宇宙线也可能与超新星的爆炸有关，然而天体物理学家并不确定。不过无论真相如何，恐怕都非常糟糕，你想必也不想卷入其中。

　　科学家们通过使用"云室"[1]（一种可以拍摄这些宇宙线入射轨道的简单设备），发现了大量令人眼花缭乱的基本粒子，这些粒子比在原子中发现的那些更加先进，每个粒子具有不同的质量、荷和自旋。紧接着在 1946 年 10 月和 1947 年 5 月，两起意外事件的发生似乎揭示了某些从未发现过的粒子。

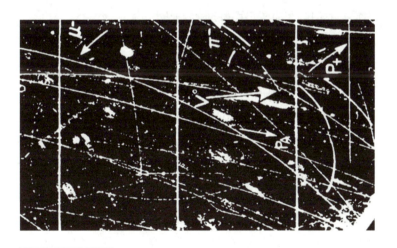

1　云室是一种简单装置，通过突然降低饱和蒸汽的压力来探测宇宙线粒子进入云室的路径，粒子的轨迹能够使得液滴从蒸汽中凝结出来。这些液滴在入射粒子的路径上被电离成核，这些液滴的照片可以揭示粒子的轨迹。粒子的性质可以通过对云室施加电场或磁场，观察它们对粒子路径的影响来进行研究。云室是由一位在本尼维斯山工作的苏格兰气象学家于 1911 年发明的，云室在 20 世纪 30 至 40 年代发现亚原子粒子的过程中发挥了关键作用，这一发现最终形成了夸克理论。

在曼彻斯特发现这些粒子的研究人员发布了上面的这张照片，你一眼就能看到，这张照片十分清晰地显示了一种叫做 K 介子的物质穿过云室的轨迹。科学家用一个小小的白色箭头标出了这条轨迹，这个小箭头本身几乎无法辨认，并与另外四个箭头混合在一起，插入这四个箭头似乎是为了将 K 介子与其他粒子来个鱼目混珠。显然，物理学家永远不会放过任何一个开玩笑的机会。

根据当时公认的理论，这种 K 介子粒子应该在十万亿分之一秒内衰减。然而照片中观察到的寿命实际为预期的一万亿倍。科学家无法解释这种粒子是如何持续这么长时间的，因而他们称这种情况为"奇异"。因此，奇异性便成为基本粒子物理学的基础思想之一。物理学家开始思考这样一种可能性：除了质量、荷和磁自旋这些能够在人类世界中被观察到的基本属性外，可能存在类似"奇异性"这种没有直接体现在感观层面的亚原子粒子固有的其他基本属性。

随着时间的推移，实验人员发现了一个庞大且不断扩大的粒子家族，并将它们命名为"强子"[1]，意思是"强大的粒子"。这个粒子家族包括质子、中子（它们与电子一起组成原子）、K 介子以及其他许多奇异粒子，如来自外层空间的 π 介子。在强子家族中发现大量新粒子后，科学家们就开始尝试让它们形

1　强子一词来源于 αδρός 或 hadrós，意思是"强大的"或"厚的"。它们是由夸克组成的复合粒子，由强力聚集在一起，这有点像分子，但是在亚原子粒子水平上的。人们在对撞机中对强子进行了研究，大型强子对撞机包含约一万个冷却到-270°C 的超导磁体，完美地安放在日内瓦附近的圆形地下隧道中，隧道周长为 27 公里。大型强子对撞机耗资约 132.5 亿美元。这些对撞机将铅等重元素的原子核以略低于光速的速度撞在一起，然后研究从它们身上飞出的残骸。

成某种秩序。科学家们发现，如果他们假设所有强子实际上都是由更小的粒子组合而成，那么就可以解释为何强子会按照相似的属性和质量聚集。对这些粒子进行排序最成功的方法叫做"八正法"，是由加利福尼亚州的物理学家盖尔曼教授于 1961 年发明的。盖尔曼提出在云室中显示的所有粒子都是他称为"夸克"[1] 的东西的组合，并将这些想法发展为粒子物理学的标准模型，现在这个模型可以解释宇宙中所有已观察到的粒子，这些粒子都是由六种基础夸克中的两种或三种组合而成的。对于粒子物理学家而言，这是一个惊人的成就，而盖尔曼本人最终也因此项工作获得了诺贝尔奖。（别丧气，我保证再写几页就完了。）

盖尔曼教授和他的同事们将这六种类型的夸克称为：

上、下、奇、魅、美、真[2]

夸克不能单个进行观察，因为它们之间的吸引力并不随着距离的增加而减少。[3]当夸克彼此分离时，他们周围的能量变

1　盖尔曼想到这个有意思的词是从詹姆斯·乔伊斯那里得到的灵感。乔伊斯写了《芬尼根的守灵夜》，这本书即使是对量子物理学家来说都很难懂。出于某种原因，乔伊斯写了这样一句话："冲马克王叫三声夸克。他一定没有从一声吼叫中得到什么，他所有的东西肯定是在这个痕迹之外。"
2　夸克理论首次提出时，后两种类型被称为"美"和"真"，缩写为"B 夸克"和"T 夸克"。随着时间推移，二者的名称有所改变，如今更常见的是把 B 夸克叫做"底夸克（bottom）"，T 夸克叫做"顶夸克（top）"。我在此处使用的是旧时的称呼。
3　这就是所谓的色禁闭。这意味着夸克不能被单独分离出来，因此不能直接观察到（见下页注 1）。夸克聚集在一起形成强子。强子有两种类型，分别叫做介子（一个夸克，一个反夸克）和重子（三个夸克），比如质子和中子。组成母强子的夸克不能从母强子中分离出来，这就是为什么目前夸克不能以更直接的方式进行研究或观察，而要以强子的形式组合起来进行观察研究，这个事实还不能用理论来解释。

28

得十分巨大，以至于能够在时空中立即产生另一对夸克-反夸克组合。因此，夸克永远是成群结队的，并且只能在由夸克聚合成的强子中观察到。[1]

夸克不能单独进行观察，只能通过观察它们的组合的行为来进行推断。夸克只有在集体行动时才能被感知，也只有在更大的背景下才有意义。在我们的世界中，永远无法直接观察上、下、奇、魅、美、真这六种夸克的个体属性，因为它们被自然界[2]绑在一起，不可分割。

现在我们来到了关键点。中国诗歌就像夸克一样，或者像汉字的偏旁一样，不能孤立地呈现，也不能孤立地理解。它们必须组合成一个整体，放到一定的语境中，并且即便是这样，他们仍然带有不确定性。数学家们可能会对这样的类比表示抗议，量子色动力学[3]和唐代诗歌之间显然没有可比性。到底有没有呢？

每当读到关于亚原子物理学的东西时，我仿佛看到那些了不起的人们，那些兢兢业业的科学家们在粒子对撞机旁埋头苦干。当他们深入研究亚原子粒子的内在时，一定也能感受到那种神秘，谁会感受不到呢？

或许我们也应该大开脑洞，接受这种人类知识边界的神奇。例如，诺贝尔奖获得者莱昂·莱德曼将上帝和希格斯玻

1　在大爆炸后几毫秒内的极端恶劣环境下，可能确实存在自由夸克。负责大型强子对撞机和布鲁克黑文的质子同步加速器的科学家们都认为，在以光速的 99.99999% 的速度将铅原子核撞击在一起后，他们可能看到了这一物质阶段，即夸克胶子等离子体。人们能做到这个程度真是不可思议。布鲁克黑文的碰撞发生在 4 万亿摄氏度，而日内瓦附近的大型强子对撞机则达到了 5.5 万亿摄氏度。

2　或者其实是胶子，但我们不谈这个了。

3　量子色动力学是对夸克相互作用的一种数学描述，很难理解。

色子[1]联系起来，这惹恼了他的一些物理学同人，因为后来希格斯玻色子在大众媒体上被称为上帝粒子。但是物理学家并不需要选择用"魅"或"奇"来描述某种类型的夸克，盖尔曼教授最初提出他的夸克模型时也没必要选择"夸克"这个怪异又难懂的词，更不需要根据古代佛经的《八正道》[2]把他的理论命名为八正法。另外，霍金教授也不是被迫写道，假如把四大基本力统一在了万有理论中，那么我们可能会"摸透上帝的意志"。但是对于他们这样的描述我们都应该感到高兴，因为他们选择了这些特殊而让人回味的词语，这意味着不论是科学家还是诗人都在自己的世界里找寻自己的上帝，无论那是什么、是谁，[3]他们都在找寻自己的真理，无论那有多么难以琢磨。而他们所选用的语言意味着就算我们只是在探寻中国古代诗歌的旅途中做短暂的停留，也能够体会这般奇异的感觉，一睹亚原子粒子物理世界的奇妙之境。

1　希格斯玻色子是粒子物理学标准模型中的基本粒子，它体现了希格斯场的量子激发。希格斯场的存在在大型强子对撞机中得到了证实，解释了为什么基于控制基本粒子相互作用的对称性，基本粒子应该是没有质量的，但是其实有一些基本粒子是有质量的。

2　《八正道》是写于历史发展早期的一本指南，其中列出了佛教的修行，可以引导人们从死亡和重生的轮回中解脱出来。《八正道》教导我们，一个人通过约束自己、培养自律、练习正念和冥想，可以达到涅槃，从而结束导致所有痛苦的渴望、执着和业力的累积。

3　例如，爱因斯坦似乎相信泛神论或是全能的上帝，即神性以一种奇怪的类似道的方式存在于整个现实之中，而不是一个具有干涉主义意志的、拟人化的上帝。他还称自己是不可知论者而非无神论者。另一方面，狄拉克预言了反物质的存在，因为他注意到在定义质量的方程中，平方根既可以是正的也可以是负的。作为一个无神论者，他坚持数学真理的标准是美。就我个人而言，我觉得克莱门特·艾德礼在这个问题上的观点最有说服力。当人们问他是不是不可知论者时，他的回答是："我不知道！"

六　中国历史概论

如果中国的诗歌和诗人就像夸克一样，只能通过整体组合起来，并置于更广阔的语境中才能被理解，那么这种语境又是什么呢？

我希望大家能允许我花点时间先搭一下架子。首先，我想概括介绍中国，包括中国最重要的主题和事件。然后，我将逐步展开这些诗人生活的特定时期，并借鉴爱因斯坦相对论的命名法，为我们在这个特定时空的旅程建立一个"参考框架"。我将试着用关于中国诗歌的一种特殊理论作为结尾，我们拭目以待吧。

我们先通过三组观察来构建中国历史概论。

观察之一：我应当从起源开始讲，因为从头开始往往是一个良好的开端。至于源头到底在哪里，每个人的观点可能都不同，但是如果我们在西方文明的 t=0 附近寻找，或许《创世记》的第一章是不错的选择。如果我们这样选的话，圣詹姆斯版本的《圣经》或许是最合适的：

"起初，神创造天地。地是空虚混沌。渊面黑暗。神的灵运行在水面上。神说，要有光，就有了光。神看

光是好的，就把光暗分开了。神称光为昼，称暗为夜。有晚上，有早晨，这是头一日。"

透过这些词句，我们立即把人与一个人格化并能够干涉人间的神联系了起来。如果我们进一步探寻这个故事，便会发现，神通过教会来回应人们的祷告，教会不时宣称所有与神的沟通交流都必须通过教会。[1]

那么，如果我们把目光转向东方，寻找中国文明中 t=0 的时刻，我们又该选择什么呢？或许是《论语》的首篇？让我们听听孔子是怎么说的：

> 学而时习之，不亦说乎
>
> 有朋自远方来，不亦乐乎
>
> 人不知而不愠，不亦君子乎

不论何时何地何人，孔子的这些思想都一定能被认同吗？也许上面两个对比选段恰好体现了中国和西方的一个基本区别。[2] 在西方，对于人与上帝的关系仿佛已经形成了某些默认的原则，这些原则虽然不容争辩，但却需要在各种具体的情况之下辩来论去，因为宗教强调要有信仰的飞跃。而在中国，办实事才是头等大事。外国人可能会花上好几个小时思考超脱之事，或是只顾讨论原则，有时根本不在意结果，或者对"这是一张桌子吗？"的确切含义进行哲学思考，与

1　试想一下，任何一部符合情理的反垄断法会对此做出什么反应。

2　顺便说一句，《圣经》中当然有很多谚语和寓言，但没有像在《论语》里那样把它们放在中心和开头的位置。

此同时，中国的先贤们或许正和朋友围桌酣饮，不醉不归。[1]
相比于做出最初选择的指导原则，中国人似乎更注重实际行
动的效果；中国人更关心的是结果，而不是为了达到目的而
必须遵守的死理。中国人的思想是否更贴近边沁的功利主义
而不是康德的道德律令？[2] 或者按照中文的说法："不管黑猫白
猫，会抓老鼠就是好猫。"

那么我的第一个总结是，西方人倾向于固守原则，而中国
人更看重结果，遵循"实践是检验真理的唯一标准"这一准则。

观察之二：我想说的第二点并非什么实证研究的结果，
而是我在中国生活多年的感悟，那就是与西方相比，历史似
乎在中国现代社会的运行中发挥着更大的作用。中国人似乎
有比我们更强的集体记忆，也因此与过往有更深的联系。[3]生活
在中国，你会感觉到历史以一种西方无法比拟的方式影响着
现代社会的方方面面[4]，这一特点可能来自于书面文字的性质。

1　这绝对不是对中国人思想的轻视，而更像是思想的解放。毕竟，尽管他
们常常喝得酩酊大醉——这真叫人赞叹，但中国人建立了历史上持续时
间最长，甚至可以说是最成功的国家。再说了，柏拉图的朋友们在他的
《会饮篇》中也都喝得醉醺醺的。
2　或者，就像我儿子曾经在酒吧里问的那样，中国人是不是更像"结果主
义者而不是义务论者"，不管这两个词是什么意思。他后来解释说，义
务论的意思是"以原则为指导，而不太在乎结果是不是有益的"。我儿
子的这种说法表面上看起来颇为耐心，但我后来却发现这不过是他无情
的拖延战术，只是想要在我这里再骗几瓶啤酒喝罢了。
3　我承认，这种记忆有时是有选择性的，取决于统治者，即胜利者，毕
竟，历史是由胜利者来书写的。
4　我也承认这里存在一个矛盾，中国人几乎摧毁了他们古代文化的所有物
质表现形式，而像埃及人，则在相当程度上保留了他们古代文化的物质
表现形式。但是我想说，中国人认为他们的古代思想对于解决当今广泛
存在的问题有直接的实操性，而埃及人、希腊人和意大利人却不使用他
们的古代思想来解决当代的危机。

我们看到，由于没有动词时态，汉语与过去保持着很强的联系，但还有一个重要因素是构成汉语这门语言的汉字。与现代欧洲语言不同的是，每个汉字与过去的联系都十分紧密。汉字与字母表不同，汉字代表的不仅仅是发音，而且是完整的意思，因此抵御了时间和地区的侵蚀。[1]汉字的发音可能会随着时间的推移而发生变化，而且各地方言不同，但一个个写下来的汉字是不变的。"涕"这个字可能有 ti、di 或 tsi 的发音，但它的意思总是鼻涕。[2]与发音不同，这些字历经千年，含义依然可辨，正是它们让历史鲜活了起来。早在公元前六世纪，中国哲学家便开始用竹简记录自己的想法，他们使用的许多汉字至今仍在使用，比如"道"。[3]这就好像，只要稍加努力，柏拉图或亚里士多德的话就会从原文中蹦出来。

直至上个世纪，过去与现在之间的联系一直通过传统的记年法得以加强，这种记年法很难判定相对的历史时期。年份是由皇帝的年号决定的，比如嘉庆十八年是公元 1813 年，而乾德三年是公元 965 年，但这之间没有任何东西表明其中一个日期比另一个早了 848 年。过去似乎融进了现在，周而复始，永无止境，既没有明确的时间发展轴，也没有一个 t=0 的

1　这在二十世纪五十年代繁体字简化的时候被打断了，比如"雲"写作"云"，"靈"写作"灵"，简化的目的是为了扫盲。这种做法把汉语和其古代起源的联系破坏了一部分。

2　这并不是说汉语是一成不变的。一些汉字的含义在不断演变，而有一些汉字则不再使用，就像英文中的 counterpane 或 wainscot，但古汉语比古英语更容易理解。甚至有人可能会问，八世纪的时候英文有哪些书面形式？不论有哪些，除了专家以外，如今我们已经无法理解它们了。

3　"道路""渠道"，还有老子和庄子所教导的"道"。

34

精确源头。

汉字除了把历史化作钢印，与表音文字不同，它的表义性质还有另外两种结果。首先，中国政府能管理世界上最大的疆域是因为即使发音不同，来自中央的命令也能下达至千里之外并被准确理解。另外，通过将艺术与意义相结合，汉字鼓励了文人阶层的兴起，从而提供了一大批受过良好教育的人才来管理这样一个庞大而复杂的国家。这两点——文字跨越千山万水促成指令上传下达，以及由受过良好教育的文人组成的官僚机构的发展[1]——促进了规模经济和大量权力集中到一个人手里。纵观历史，在和平稳定时期，除了朝廷的派系之外，中国内部传统意义上很少有相互制衡的权力中心。没有教会[2]、议会、司法机关，也没有贵族能够占地为王，并强大到拥有组建军队的实力。尽管皇帝的龙椅有时坐得并不算稳，但是整个国家的权力掌握在"一人"手中。历史赋予了中国政府特殊的角色，使其行使无限的权力。

既然我们已经猜到了皇权至高无上的原因，那么我们现在需要想想是什么让中国政府得以运转。这些线索可以再次从历史中找到，政府的基本心思颇为直白，一切都可以归结为自上而下，维护统一。两千多年来，中国历经了王朝的迭代兴衰，合久而分，分久而合。在秩序井然的时代，经济繁

1　这里可能还有另一个因素，那就是由于书面语较为复杂，因此阻止了那些未受过教育的阶层与可能动摇国体的重要群体进行交流和接触。有人说，纵观中国历史，没有一个王朝是由读过《孙子兵法》的农民建立的，起义通常是由饥民和文盲发起的，毕竟他们没有什么可以失去了，这么做也毫不稀奇。

2　事实上，佛教"教会"在公元840-849年发展十分强劲，招致唐武宗发动了一场可怕的大清洗。武宗发布律令称："我们将根除这种瘟疫……。"

荣，艺术蓬勃发展，国际化的都市随着商业和贸易而兴起，能工巧匠辈出，制作出各式陶器、铁器、玉器，伟大的作家和哲学家们熠熠生辉，画家的笔下色彩愈发绚烂。书法家制作了精美的狐毛笔[1]，粮仓里堆满了食物，中华民族尽享和平的福祉。然后中央权力逐渐腐败，赋税在转运到首都途中被转移，贪官污吏压榨百姓，无视惩戒，陷入了堕落的生活。最终，洪泛区的堤坝无人修复，粮仓沦为废墟，自然灾害频发而政府无力应对。中央权力逐渐减弱，最终完全坍塌。帝国陷入深渊，经历了大约一个世纪的战争、饥荒、疾病、洪水和难以想象的苦难。最终总会有一个农民战士揭竿而起，随着好战本能的觉醒，杀伐果断，将这个破碎的王国拼凑在一起，新的循环再次开始。

观察之三：我的第三点想法是，中国广阔疆土长期的大一统促进了大量文化和文明资产以及物质财富的积累，从而引起了外界的嫉妒。很明显，在某些时期，比如公元八世纪初期，中国确实比当时世界上任何国家都更有吸引力。因此，长期以来，中华民族从根本上形成了一种防御性而非侵略性的性格。[2]

长城从很多方面而言都可以看作是中国最强大、最普遍的象征，也是中国国歌中的核心主题。如果我们去试想西方世界中类似的有力象征，并不能找到一个完全对等的实体结构，或许十字架勉强可以算一个吧。虽然对不同的人来说，十字架所代表的意义各不相同，但西方宗教的一个重要方面

1　最好的画笔是用兔毛制成的，敏锐的读者可能会在第 110 页第四行注意到这点。
2　然而，中国也曾爆发旨在收复唐朝鼎盛时期领土的战争，代价高昂。

是劝教、传教，让其他社会接受西方的观点，而长城的防御性特征则是彻头彻尾毫无争议的。基辛格在描述这一区别时写道，西方主张道德例外主义，而中国主张文明例外主义。这一论述看似简单实际上内容丰富，或许可以解释为什么一些西方国家热衷于在本国领土之外进行军事和殖民探索，而中国人似乎更满足于现状。

下一章中我们绘制"参考框架"时将要参考的时代恰恰展示了上述稳定和混乱的循环往复。公元 618 年，唐朝的建立给这个经历了几个世纪动乱和苦难的国家带来了法律和秩序，接下来的一个半世纪里中国经历了"教育的黄金时代"，诗人和画家大放异彩，外国人纷纷涌入首都，唐朝都城也成为世界上最大、最国际化的城市[1]，聚集着来自世界各地的商人。公元 712 年至公元 756 年，唐明皇统治时期唐朝达到鼎盛。彼时天下太平，诗仙诗圣俱在。然而，皇帝逐渐厌倦了政事，大臣们渐渐懈怠。唐明皇沉迷于杨贵妃的美色中不能自拔，并任由贵妃亲信安禄山，一个可能是土耳其后裔的胖将军，掌管了北方三大要塞的军队。公元 755 年，安禄山叛乱，夺取了当时中国的第二大城市洛阳。朝廷历经一番权力斗争后，指派了一位无能的将军来应对安禄山的大军，安军很快突破了一个重要关口，向首都挺进。皇帝吓得惊慌失措，匆匆逃往西边。逃亡的第二天，士兵们团团围住玄宗，要求赐死杨贵妃，并指责杨贵妃是这场灾难的罪魁祸首。伤心欲绝的玄宗被迫同意处死杨贵妃，杨贵妃被大太监勒死在附近的庙里。皇帝此后元气大伤，再也没有恢复，余生都在思念他的爱人，

1　长安，位于今天中国西北部的西安市内。

充满了无尽的悲痛，但这却成为一代代诗人灵感的源泉。[1]

经过一系列的持久战，叛乱在公元763年结束，但由于叛乱对政治经济造成了巨大破坏，唐朝国力大大削弱，不复从前。公元754年的人口普查中记录有5300万人，但十年后另一次普查显示只有1700万人，这其中的差距很可能在于隐匿的人口，或者是因为流离失所或战乱死亡的人数。历史学家对安禄山叛乱造成的死亡人数争论不休，但极有可能这个人数超过了第一次世界大战的死亡数量，并且相比之下占据了更大的人口比例。然而，在第一次世界大战中，是由于坦克、机关枪和有毒气体而造成了伤亡，但在安史之乱中，所有的伤亡都是由长矛、斧头、锤子、攻城机、石弩和从山上滚下来的装满石头的竹笼造成的。

在中国漫长的历史中，这样的灾难每隔一段时间便会发生一次，以至于有"大乱"[2]这样一个专门的词来形容这种极端而持久的混乱，这在我们的语言中是不存在的。王朝起起伏伏，兴兴衰衰，就像一道巨大的正弦波贯穿了中国的历史。我们看到了建立于公元前206年的汉朝的兴衰，然后是短命的隋朝，之后是唐、宋、元、明、清，每一个朝代都持续了大约三个世纪，朝代交替间往往历经极端困苦，直到1911年最后一个王朝崩溃。[3]在最近一次这样的循环中，即自19世纪50

1　这一系列事件被记录在《长恨歌》中，这首诗从第204页开始，虽然它比《伊利亚特》或《奥德赛》短得多，但要比多数中国诗歌长太多了。

2　大乱不仅指无政府状态，而且是一场全面战争，就像卢旺达或阿勒颇的战争，不过范围波及整个大陆。斯大林格勒战役和希特勒对列宁格勒发起的围攻或许可以算是大乱，但是地域范围有限，而且时间相对较短，地狱般的日子只持续了162天和872天，而不是几十年。

3　元朝寿命较短，只持续了一个世纪。

年代中期起，中国历经了近百年的大乱，直到最后一位伟大的农民革命家统一中国，并因此跻身公元前以来古老的哲人领袖之列。

正因如此，中国政府的基本任务在于维持稳定，尽可能避免发生新的"大乱"。这种稳定与大乱的交替循环也解释了为什么与西方相比，在中国，社会稳定和集体责任是压倒一切的。[1] 这些便是大体背景，现在我们继续前进，直到抵达所选诗人所处的特定时代。

39

Translation of Introduction 前言译文

---

1 我并不想评判对错，但是我认为解释和理解其原因是十分重要的。

七　参考框架

　　前文大致介绍了中国的历史，本章将重点介绍诗人们生活的唐宋时期，这一时期在中国历史上横跨了公元 618 年至公元 1279 年间的六个半世纪，催生了中华上下五千年里最伟大最繁荣的文学与艺术。历史上有哪个国家的哪一段时期像唐宋这般富有创造力、充满活力而又高产呢？无论这个问题的答案是什么，我们都将用这一时期为接下来的旅程建立我们的参考框架。不难发现，唐宋在有序和混乱之间跌宕，国家经历了几十年的动荡，人们生活在饥饿、暴乱和随时可能丢掉性命的恐惧之中。然而浩瀚的中国文学是贯穿这一时期的主线，也是贯穿和联结整个中国历史，使其能够在政治经济全面崩溃后存活下来的主线。

唐

　　唐朝是由李渊建立的，李渊是中国北方城市太原的最高长官和家族族长。公元 617 年，李渊在女儿的支持下起义。李渊之女组建了自己的军队，治军非常严格。李渊于公元 618 年 6 月 18 日称帝，此后不久，他的儿子李世民[1]杀掉了两个同

1　我曾经去过李世民的陵墓昭陵，在陕西乾县附近。那天早晨一直在下大雨，我全身都湿透了。最后我放弃了骑自行车，打了一辆出租车，沿着一

胞兄弟，并将李渊罢黜了。李世民便是唐太宗，继李渊之后，他带领唐朝进入了和平繁荣的太平盛世。唐朝在随后一个世纪中唐明皇四十四年统治下的前半期达到鼎盛。

鼎盛时期的唐朝代表了中华文明的一个顶峰。透过历史的迷雾，唐朝看起来似乎是一个秩序井然的和谐社会，皇帝仁慈，虽严厉却富有爱心。我相信现实要复杂得多，但是，至今初唐仍被视作一个和平安定、繁荣昌盛的时代，以其丰富的休闲活动而闻名，比如宴会、饮酒、旅游、狩猎、射箭，甚至是那古里古怪的拔河运动。官员们休假时去看望父母或主持孩子的婚礼，人人都享有作为法定节假日的春节、元宵节和寒食节。此外，人们还举行盛会来庆祝军事胜利、丰收和皇帝大赦天下。公元 664 年的一次盛宴聚集了一千多名老人，而公元 768 年的另一次宴会则有三千多名官员参加，不久以后皇帝还为一千二百名妇女举行了宴会。那个时候，豪饮几乎被视为一种美德。[1]

唐朝都城长安呈棋盘状，其中皇宫在中轴线上稍稍偏北。在其他地方则分布着寺庙、神龛和修道院，诵经的僧侣口中念念有词，铁制香炉里升起袅袅青烟，飘荡在庙宇上方。佛

Translation of Introduction 前言译文

（接上页）条蜿蜒的小路上山。一路上云雾缭绕，我们周围的山谷里全是潮湿的雾气。我们到达昭陵的时候，雾太大了，什么都看不清，于是我想让司机带我回酒店，但他坚持让我去看看。我找到废弃的检票口走了进去，沿着一条小路，穿过一片浓密的松树林，路上看到了石头做的香炉，最后爬了几级湿滑的台阶，上到一处高台上。在浓浓的雾气中，我的眼前赫然耸立着一个李世民的巨大雕像，雕像两侧各有三根云柱。李世民似乎在往前倾，朝我这边倒过来。我在那里站了很久，凝视着眼前巨大的雕像。风刮过松树林，传来飒飒的风声，石板被雨水冲刷以后折射出惨白的幽灵般的光，眼前的雕像忽隐忽现，似乎也在随光晃动。

1 但这并非举止粗野，而是为了倡导思想自由。

教已经传入中国，并被定为官方信仰。[1]

在政府监管的市场中，商人们出售大麦、大豆、萝卜、杏、桃、盐、大蒜、栗子和核桃。饭馆里有猪肉、鸡肉、羊肉、海獭、骆驼，甚至还有熊，不过这东西显然不容易弄到。佳肴鲜美，如牡蛎（配上美酒）、马蹄蟹和河豚（当地人称之为"河仔猪"）都是现捞的。高级酒馆和妓院里都有受过严格的餐桌礼仪培训的妓女，她们应对规则复杂的酒桌游戏时也是得心应手。当时那些受过教育的女性似乎十分受尊重。据史料记载，她们不怕直斥男人们令人难以忍受的无聊谈话破坏了宴会的雅兴，甚至在碰到酒醉之徒动手动脚时会狠狠地拧他们的耳朵。确实，那个时候也出现了中国历史上被唯一的女皇帝武则天统治的一段时间。

在这种国际化的氛围中，艺术蓬勃发展，造纸术、养蚕业、青瓷高温上釉、篆刻艺术、绘画、书法、壁画装饰艺术、陶瓷、漆器雕刻等也达到鼎盛。与此同时，唐朝也产生了中国历史上一些最伟大的诗歌。

然而，公元755年安禄山叛乱使得王朝支离破碎。如前所述，尽管政权幸存了下来，却受到极大削弱，以至于不得不放弃对农业和商业的掌控。到公元845年，有记载称强盗和河盗在长江沿岸大肆抢掠，而军队毫无抵抗之力。公元858年，大运河泛滥成灾，许多人认为唐朝天命已尽。[2] 而一场可怕的

---

1 我们不应忘记第35页（"前言译文"部分）的注释。

2 所谓天命，是用来证明皇权合法性的原则，但天命是有代价的。人们相信天命只能授予公正的统治者，这个统治者必须通过以德治国来获得这样的天命；如果统治者不履行义务，做一个道德的和称职的统治者，那么他就失去了天命的授权，从而也就失去了做皇帝的资格。人们普遍认为，天降大灾，如饥荒和洪水，是一个王朝走向灭亡的征兆。

饥荒更是在公元 873 年将这个毫无应对之力的帝国逼到了崩溃的边缘。紧接着直到公元 907 年唐朝最终覆灭之前，中国还经历了一段割据和混战时期。按照那可怕而不可避免的循环，中国陷入了长达五十年的动荡和灾难期，即五代十国，最终在宋朝得以重新统一。从公元 960 年到公元 1279 年，宋朝走过了三个世纪。

宋

宋朝就像唐朝一样可以分为两个时期，但宋朝的情况略有不同，它的分割是由外族入侵而不是内部叛乱造成的。外族入侵迫使宋朝永久迁都，从北方的开封搬到杭州。杭州是一大文化中心，地处南方，沿湖而建，离现在的上海很近。因此，宋朝划分为两个时期：公元 960 年到公元 1127 年为北宋，公元 1127 年到公元 1279 年为南宋。宋朝时期，人口翻了一番，从一亿增加到两亿，而我们的诗人们要么生活在北宋初期，要么亲历了叛乱。

宋朝的第一位皇帝宋太祖一统天下后，致力于改革科举制度[1]，完善驿站系统，并编制了一份覆盖所有主要行政中心的地图集，希望以此来加强国家的统一。

宋代中国的社会生活堪与盛唐比肩。鉴赏家们热衷于高

43

Translation of Introduction 前言译文

（接上页）因此，在重大环境事件发生后，经常发生叛乱，因为这些事件被视为上天的怒意。例如，1626 年 5 月 30 日早晨，北京城西南隅的王恭厂发生了一场神秘的大爆炸，造成两万余人死亡，北京城大部分地区遭到巨大破坏，影响范围达三万米，不过爆炸基本没有引发火灾。大爆炸发生后，很多人都指责是天启皇帝迷恋木工，荒疏政事，因而触怒了上天。

1 唐朝的崩溃摧毁了帝国官僚体制中的贵族阶层。

雅艺术品的交易，木刻板印刷术和后来的活字印刷术的发明促进了文学的传播。为了跟上时代的步伐，朱熹等哲学家通过集注和重修主要文本的方式复兴了儒家思想。在其鼎盛时期，宋朝曾是地球上最大、最富有的国家。通过引进来自中亚的早熟品种，水稻种植得以推广，这使得国家能够在皇仓体系中生产和储存富余的粮食。此外，宋朝还建立了养老院、公共诊所和贫民公墓。妇女享有一定的财产权，许多女子以其受到的精良教育和文学成就而闻名，尽管这并非实现性别平等的灵丹妙药。在城市里，既有木偶戏表演者、耍蛇人，也有杂技演员、吞剑者和随着木拍子有节奏的敲打声吟诵诗歌的人[1]，就像中世纪的说唱歌手，茶馆和能够容纳千人的剧院随处可见。

十二世纪初的一幅著名卷轴描绘了宋都一天的生活。这幅名为《清明上河图》的卷轴随着时空流转，就像云室里的轨迹一样，在黎明时分从卷轴的最右边开始，渔船静静地驶入河中。当眼睛向左移动时，我们沿着河岸追随着一日光景。到了午餐时分，我们到达了一座挤满人的虹桥，桥的位置正好是卷轴正中，桥上插满了旗子，桥周围是忙碌的餐馆，供应着冒着热气的饺子。天色稍暗的时候，在更靠左的地方，茶馆里挤满了客人。在我们即将结束卷轴一日游时，一排骆驼商队从一座宏伟的大门下缓缓走出，开启一段漫长的旅程。[2]

1　我曾于1988年在西安看过类似的表演，现在陕西农村地区还有这样的表演。

2　卷轴宽10英寸，长近6码。卷轴里描绘了八百人、二十八艘船、六十种动物、三十幢建筑物，还有许多树木和车轿。河流蜿蜒穿过整幅画卷。在城外的田野里，有悠闲的乡里人，如农民、牧羊人、养猪人。通往城市的主干道联结着众多乡间小路。远方，工人们把

在各地，法律是由不断流动的行政长官和训练有素的法官来执行的，他们所用的惩罚措施包括狠狠鞭打双脚和用竹竿杖打臀部。刑事案件中使用了新的法医技术来确定受害者是否有被勒死、溺水、被毒打或中毒的迹象。

在高雅文学和民间文学中，诗歌都成为主要的表达方式，并被编成规模宏大的诗集，如《千家诗》，还有史学和政治专著，例如《资治通鉴》。《资治通鉴》于公元 1084 年出版，总结了宋朝之前的十一个朝代的历史，全书共 294 卷。八个世纪后，毛泽东反复阅读该书，在他的大床边堆满了这部书，他不断从中寻找意义，直到生命的尽头。[1]

到了十一世纪中叶，宋代经济和社会运动的爆发给当时中国的政治阶层带来了巨大的压力，稳定与混乱这一不可避免的循环慢慢转动着。社会的日益复杂引发了朝廷关于政策的激烈争论。官僚机构改制的尝试与建立政府对盐的垄断来

（接上页）货物装到船上，商店柜台上堆满了待出售的货物，甚至还能看到税务局。卷轴里有小贩、杂耍艺人、演员、乞丐、僧侣、算命师、医生、旅店老板和木匠。在桥上，一艘大船的桅杆仍在升起，却几近失控，引发了巨大骚动。有人向下面的船员扔下绳索，桥上的人群对着船打着手势大声呼喊。这可能是中国最著名的画作了，被称为中国的《蒙娜丽莎》，尽管这二者的主题和技巧完全不同。这幅卷轴笔触生动，画上的动作令人惊叹，细节处描绘了在遥远过去的复杂世界里普通人的生活，可以久久地吸引人们的注意力。我曾经从北京飞到香港去看《清明上河图》的特展，这幅画大约五年才展出一次。等到我赶到美术馆，才发现未来六周的票都已经售完了。香港有六百万人口，而许多排队参观的人只有十几岁。

1　在《资治通鉴》成书的同时，《天工开物》一书总结了宋朝在技术、数学、哲学、科学和工程方面取得的巨大进步。尽管这本书在明朝末期才得以出版，但书中的很多发明都来自宋朝。这本百科全书式的作品涵盖众多技能，包括灌溉、养蚕、汞的提取、制盐、冶金、造纸，当然还有发酵饮料。

间接提高税收和重新分配财富引起了保守派的强烈反对。[1] 焦灼且旷日持久的权力斗争分散了朝廷的注意力,大大削弱了朝廷的力量,直到公元 1127 年 1 月 9 日,一支庞大的叛军从北方涌入,洗劫了宋都。这支叛军是女真部落的后裔金人指挥的,他们最初居住在极其东北的森林里和河岸边。叛军一路南下穿越中国,同时俘虏了宋钦宗及其父宋徽宗,宋徽宗是被叛军吓得退位的,朝廷被迫逃往南方城市杭州。在之后的十年里,南宋持续着抗金之战,最终双方于公元 1141 年签订了和约。宋朝都城由开封迁至杭州,成为北宋与南宋的分界线。

尽管宋朝失去了对黄河流域这一中华文明发祥地的控制,但其经济依然强劲,宋朝仍然拥有庞大的人口和中国大部分富饶的耕地。宋朝利用这些财富,建造了用于国内和海上贸易的船只,并建设了带有灯塔和仓库的巨大港口。公元 1161年,在长江上的一次战斗中,宋朝首次使用了明轮船,并配备了巨大的配重弹射器,向敌人发射了威力强大的火药炸弹。将士们配备了能够喷出火焰和发射弹片的"火枪"。宋朝的军事能力大大增强,武器库中摆满了爆炸手榴弹、大炮和地雷。

与此同时,宋朝通过改革和加强科举,增强了对合格官员的聘用。这些举措帮助中国从一个由将军和权势家族精英主导的社会,转变为一个由更有能力、受过良好教育、德行出众的文人,或"士大夫"统治的社会。宋朝时人们还成立

---

1 当八百年之后的卡尔·马克思坐在大英图书馆时,他一定会对此表示赞同。国外文献中多次提到宋朝著名丞相王安石曾写道:"国家应该把工商业和农业全部掌管在自己手中,以帮扶劳动阶级,防止他们被富人踩在脚底。"遗憾的是我没有找到这句充满理想主义的话的中文原文。

了股份制合伙公司，大型船只可以通过长江和大运河运输货物，钢铁行业的冶炼厂每年产量达数百万吨，如果煤炭没有取代木炭，这些冶炼厂恐怕会消耗掉所有森林。

元

和平持续了很久，直到成吉思汗带领着他的蒙古大军越过冰冻的大草原从北方攻入。公元 1271 年，宋朝最终向成吉思汗的孙子忽必烈投降，忽必烈成为元朝的第一任皇帝，定都在靠近现在北京边界的地方。然而历史的车轮仍在转动，虽然忽必烈在他早期的皇帝生涯中心性狠厉，行动力强，但那令人熟悉的腐败和倦怠很快开始滋长。忽必烈变得异常肥胖，痛风得厉害，却还没完没了地大口吃肉，大喝马奶酒（一种由马奶发酵而成的酒）。他像唐明皇一般将国家抛之脑后，并几乎一直处于醉酒状态。在他的专属狩猎区中，他躺在镀金的轿子里包有虎皮的长沙发上，由四头大象驮着，随行的还有五百只训练来追捕熊和野猪的猎鹰、豹子和猞猁。公元 1368 年，忽必烈的王朝不可避免地遭遇了命定的坍塌。

八　中国诗歌的特殊理论

现在到了问题的关键——这些都意味着什么？为什么要关注这些事呢？

根据传说，中国最早的诗歌可以追溯到公元前二十三世纪，诗歌由简短而精练的歌曲组成，比如《击壤歌》，农民们在土地上劳作时可能会唱这首歌：

日出而作	When the sun comes out, we work,
日入而息	When it goes in, we rest.
凿井而饮	When we dig wells, we drink,
耕田而食	When we plough fields, we eat.
帝力于我何有哉	Huh! What is the Emperor's power to us?

大约两千年后，到了孔子（公元前 551 年—公元前 479 年）所在的时代，书写的传统开始发展起来，据说孔圣人自己编撰了《诗经》中的 305 首诗，《诗经》中有不知名的韵律民谣、民间故事和祭祀的诗歌。五百年后，差不多是基督时代，另一本诗集《楚辞》问世，其中收录了一些著名诗人的作品，这些作品以一种更加个性化和扣人心弦的方式

表达了人间生存的喜怒哀乐。又过了一千年，宋朝晚期诞生了另一本同样重要的诗集《千家诗》。《千家诗》是由刘克庄（1187—1269）分门别类编纂的。刘克庄选择了百花、竹木、天文、地理、宫室、气候、器用、音乐、禽兽、昆虫、时令、节候、昼夜、人品等十四类。《千家诗》出现时印刷术刚刚发明，因此这本书产生了广泛的影响，尤其是对教育系统。这三本诗集凝聚了数以万计，可能是数十万首诗歌的精髓，这些诗歌流传了数千年，影响了中国人思想的各个方面。从那时起直到现在，除了文化大革命（1966—1976）期间，对《千家诗》中经典篇目的背诵一直是学校的必修课。今天的中国学生仍然需要背诵大量的诗歌和注解，学生们在背诵的时候往往感到厌烦，但在后来的生活中，却常常能从背诵在学校里学到的诗中获得巨大的乐趣。

在这段漫长的历史进程中，诗歌已经成为定义中华文明的独一无二的艺术形式。中国在绘画、高温釉面陶瓷、建筑、戏剧、舞蹈、青铜器铸造、早期兵马俑雕刻等方面都取得了举世瞩目的成就，但诗歌是中国最具代表性的艺术形式，它跨越了时空的阻隔，所有人都能欣赏并参与进来。

"诗"这个字由两部分组成：言字旁表示"语言"，"寺"的意思是"寺院"或"寺庙"。我曾经读到[1]说这个字原本写作"誌"，由言字旁加上"志"字组成，发音为 zhì，其现代版本源自某种书法速记。这个"志"字又由两部分组成，"士"的

1　美国学者比尔·波特，笔名红松，对《千家诗》进行翻译并集结成《大师之诗》的优秀译本。我十分感激他对中国诗歌的分析，他的分析激发了我在本章中的很多想法。

意思是"学者","心"指的就是"心"。因此,"诗"这个字最初是将"学问"和"语言"的概念与"心"融合在了一起。《诗经》的序言中曾试图这样描述诗歌的概念:

在心为志　　　　　When in the heart, it's *zhì*,

发言为诗　　　　　when expressed in language, it's *shī*.

因此,从五千年前文明伊始,诗歌便承载着表达中国人内心深处的情感和信仰,以及中国人心中最深处隐秘希望的功能,它是汉字所蕴含的美和意义融合的终极升华。中文以汉字为基础的这一永恒特质为中国诗歌提供了其他文明所无法比拟的连贯性和连续性。然而,在诗歌最为核心之处,存在着一种模糊的虚无,正是这种虚无给予读者空间,使得他们能够以适合自身经历的方式来诠释诗歌的情感。尽管这些诗的中心悖论、虚无和非存在性都是按照几千年前严格的规则精心构建出来的,但它们却为读者创造了一种近乎冥想般的体验,在诗中,人间的虚无相通,而自我和外界的概念都消失了。

诗歌蕴含着中国传统文化和信仰的精髓,饱含人们对自然的亲近闲适,诉说着人类不过是广阔宇宙的一小部分,所有企图主宰自然的努力都是徒劳的。诗歌畅谈着自然力量之间的平衡转换,因此中国社会更容易接受气候变化中的人为因素。[1]诗歌中既有对不公正的愤慨,也提到了反抗不公可能会遇到的危险。上至焚书的秦始皇,下至两千年后作为哲人领袖登上权力巅峰的毛泽东,都把诗歌变成了某种武器般的存在。不过在一些更加明快的诗句中,常常可见一种温

1　中国人会问:"如果你花了两百年的时间从地下挖出数万亿吨的煤,然后烧了排放到天上,你怎么能期望大自然不会有所反应呢?"

和的、自嘲式的幽默，说明时间对于身心有着怎样的作用。我们能看到对摆脱传统的束缚，畅快呼吸新鲜空气的渴望，我们跟随着隐士，在孤独中探寻和平的足迹，想来他们刻意将自己与尘世社会和家国大事分隔开来也是愠怒到极致的一种反抗了。

在唐宋鼎盛时期，可以说没有诗歌，什么都没有意义，如果不作上几句诗作为记录，所有社交和仪式，所有个人活动和聚会都是不完整的。诗歌无处不在。直到现在，在工厂的外墙上、大街上、家里、旅馆和餐馆里、寺院里、城市广场的广告牌上都能看见诗歌。政治人物演讲爱引用诗歌，朋友或同事之间的对话也常常蹦出几句诗来阐明或弄清一个观点。诗歌既能逗人开心又能损人尊严；能说服人，也能糊弄人；能点燃忠诚之心，也能浇灭叛逆青年的怒火。所以，我们可以把这些诗作为一个窗口来打开中国人的内心世界，了解他们的思想和想象。中国人对诗歌的崇敬之情相当深厚，但凡能讲出关于诗歌的只言片语，即使不能说中文而只能通过翻译来交流，都能激发中国人民的友谊。这样你与当地人的互动一下子分量就不同了，意义也不一般了。诗歌能够更好地解释你身边发生的一切，也能增强你的理解力和同理心，还能表明你对生活体验充满兴趣，展现出你对具有普世性的东西的欣赏。用塞缪尔·约翰逊的话来说，它将给你一种"到过中国长城"的"荣光"。[1] 诗歌表达的情感是超越文化的，

1 1791 年，詹姆斯·博斯韦尔在《塞缪尔·约翰逊的一生》一书中向我们讲述了这段话的全部内容："他异常兴奋地谈论着去远方国家旅行的事，他说，心灵因旅行而变得宽广，人格因旅行而变得丰盈。他对参观

是在所有文明中都相通的，因此，诗歌与中国的日常生活有着直接的动态关联，让你能够在更深层次上进行交流。无论你想在中国做什么事，诗歌都能为你助力，也会为你赢得人气。

（接上页）中国长城的经历表达了特别的热情。我感受到了这一点（原文如此），对他说要不是我得承担照顾孩子的责任，我真的觉得我应该去看看中国的长城。'先生'他说，'如果你这样做，你可以把你的孩子培养得更加出类拔萃，因为你的精神和好奇心会给他们带来荣光，他们将永远被看作是一个到过中国长城的人的孩子。我是认真的，先生！'"

九　串连帝国的第二条线

社会在有序与混乱之间摇摆，诗歌却以其经久不衰的延续性代代相传。当诗歌将中国封建王朝的社会架构串连起来时，另一条线——科举考试制度，则将整个国家连在了一起。二者相互交织，相互促进，在很大程度上共同创造了强健的中华文明。

如前所述，诗歌的范围很广，诗中既有欢庆自然、欢颂友谊，也有悲伤的宣泄、政治斗争的刀光剑影和对爱情的美好追求。诗歌由皇帝、将军、战士、僧侣、妓女、市民和农民所作，但最重要的是，它更是由科举考试中涌现出来的文人士大夫们创作的。因此，科举对诗歌的发展产生了深远的影响，与此同时，后期的科举也反映了早期大师们的成就。

从公元前 206 年汉朝建立开始，直到上个世纪，或者可以说直到今天，在大部分时间里，治理中国的人都是通过考试选拔的。

在科举考试之前，官员是由推荐上任或是根据家族关系选拔，但汉武帝（公元前 141 年—前 87 年在位，一统天下的汉朝皇帝）使用测试技能的竞赛，开创了科举制度的雏形。真正的科举制度是在公元 605 年由短命的隋朝创立的。到了唐朝，科举制度逐步强化和改进，更加系统化，引入了策论以

及关于诗歌和其他话题的口试。公元681年，考试增加了一项要求背诵大量经典著作的科目。十二年后，由于武则天（中国唯一的女皇）需要忠于她的官员来管理官僚机构，科举考试的范围扩大到精英家族以外。随后唐朝的崩溃摧毁了强大的精英家族，巩固了科举制度作为中国社会中心支柱的地位。

随着科举考试发展为书面形式，它起到了统一文化的作用，因为是由国家来决定应该强调哪些经典文本，以及应该舍弃哪些。在随后的宋朝，科举的应试范围扩大到整个社会，许多出身低微的人通过考试成功走向高位，名声大噪。大多数人都有资格参加考试，但不时会有对各种群体的特殊限制，如巫师、乞丐、船工、性工作者和屠夫。

终试通常在都城进行，持续三天两夜。应试者被锁在单独的房间里，里面除了两块木板外什么也没有，木板可以拼成床，也可以当作书桌和长凳。应试者可以带一壶水、一个夜壶、被褥、一块砚台、墨和毛笔，在应考的三天里完全与世隔绝。如果应试者死了，会被用稻草裹起来，从考场的高墙扔出去。考生的作弊方法层出不穷，越来越巧妙。忧心忡忡的奶奶会把大量的古典文学作品勤勉地缝在孙子的内裆里，或是藏在食物中或贴身藏好。公元992年，为了杜绝普遍存在的贿赂行为，政府官员要求匿名提交试卷，但贿赂仍然存在。直到公元1105年，皇帝坚持要求誊抄答卷，这样考官便无法辨认笔迹了。

虽然科举制度能够跨越距离，凝聚人心，但它靠死记硬背照搬经典，并死死限定在八股文的传统结构中，自然抑制了创造力，所有想法都被套进了古老的枷锁中。通过统一思想，稳定社会秩序，政府达到了避免天下大乱的目的。

即便那些没通过科举考试的人也没有被抛弃。在中国古代传统思想的熏陶下，那些无法登榜的人虽然不能制定大的战略，但却被雇用负责具体的日常工作。这些人负责维护灌溉系统、堤坝和帝国粮仓，或者担任教师、税务稽查员和艺术品赞助人。

科举制度直到 1905 年才被废除，但现在中国共产党在北京颐和园旁边的干部培训学校采用的选拔最优秀干部的制度仍受到这种古老制度的影响，其目的仍然是建立一个最佳政府体系，形成一个观点相似、同盟相近的统一集体。因此，科举可能是历史上所有文明中持续时间最长的制度，也是成功治理中国这个在过去一千年里大多数时候都是地球上最大、最成功、最复杂的国家的关键因素。科举制度与诗人的成就紧密相连，科举为诗人们提供了经典的主题，但又要求他们恪守刻板的表达方式，与此同时，随着诗人们对社会的影响不断增大，科举考试也在不断变化，以适应后期的艺术发展。

十　大师们，何许人也？

本书收集的七十首诗主要写于唐宋时期，我主要关注七位诗人（六男一女[1]），还有一些其他诗人的作品也收录在内。

如前所述，中国诗歌的历史可以追溯到很早以前。在那之后许久，第一批大师才开始在四、五世纪进行创作，所以几个世纪后的唐朝诗人所代表的是诗歌的复兴，而不是根本性的思想创新。

下图展示的是七位诗人创作时期的时间轴。一如中国一

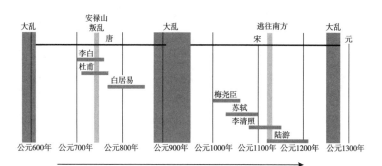

七位唐宋诗人的时间轴

1　请放心，我并不是象征性地这样选择。虽然女诗人在中国帝国时期并不少见，但出于嫉妒，许多女诗人的作品后来被男人销毁了，他们知道自己比不上那些女人。李清照的部分作品幸存了下来，并且它们属于最优秀的作品。

直以来的历史，这条时间轴上既有繁荣与和平时期，也有社会剧烈动荡的时期（即图中阴影部分）。

李白

第一个登上我们舞台的是李白（701—762）。李白号称"谪仙人"，即贬谪凡间的仙人，他的一生，不是穿梭在奇幻的自然风景中，便是在筵席上狂饮，席间他的朋友们可能会突然蹦起来，随手抓起一支毛笔，大笔一挥，便作成一幅难以辨认的书法作品。对了，他还有一种对公认的礼仪和权威的刻意蔑视。他的诗给人一种超然的感觉，以一种超凡脱俗的自由漫游世界，脚踏一条穿过荒野和自然的大道，而不是被困在社会琐事的枷锁中。不难发现，李白的大部分创作生涯都受益于稳定与和平的时代。

人们通常认为李白出生在如今的吉尔吉斯斯坦，他家在那里做贸易，生意做得很是不错。李白大约五岁的时候，他的家人搬回到中国西南部四川省的一个村庄。长在乡下，李白学会了驯养野鸟、剑术、骑马和打猎。在他二十岁之前，他曾打过仗，还杀了几个人。公元720年，他受到了知州的接见，被视为天才。或许是出于个人原因，李白从未参加过科举考试。相反，他开始了漫长的游历生涯，数年中走过许多地方，包括沿着中国的主要河流进行长途航行。到了公元740年，他似乎已经在山东定居了一段时间，并成为"竹溪六逸"之一。这是一个非正式的聚会小组，旨在欣赏文学，同时纵酒酣歌。

公元742年，李白受到唐明皇召见，在朝堂上不论是他的

作品还是他的性格都十分吸引人，尤其是他被召见的时候经常喝得醉醺醺的，但表现仍然十分出众。公元744年秋，李白结识了同为诗人的杜甫，两人因共住一屋而相识，两人都爱好打猎、旅游、饮酒、诗歌，成了亲密而长久的朋友。公元755年，安禄山叛乱让国家大乱。李白因为卷入了朝廷的阴谋斗争而被判处死刑，但在判决执行之前，一名同情他的将军用他的头衔换回了李白的性命，死刑被减为流放到偏远荒凉的甘肃省。

尽管被判流放，李白却不慌不忙地上路了，途中还进行社交拜会，其中一些持续数月，还有大吃大喝和创作活动。李白最终没能走到甘肃，而是不断游历，直到死在安徽。[1] 有个故事说，他喝得烂醉如泥与月亮的倒影交谈时，从船上掉下来，淹死了。即便这个故事不是真的，李白也可能死于他这般拼命的生活方式吧。一位著名的翻译李白诗作的美国翻译家写道：

> "几乎所有的中国诗人都歌颂饮酒的乐趣，但没有一个人像李白那样孜孜不倦、情真意切。"

杜甫

接下来要说的是杜甫（712—770）。杜甫被称作"诗圣"，许多人认为杜甫是中国历史上最伟大的诗人，他有一千五百多首诗流传至今。杜甫后期的许多诗歌涉及历史的宏大主题，也谈到了种种事件强加给人的道德困境。对自然的亲近和友

---

1 杜甫写《梦李白二首·其一》（见第222页）时，李白正因被贬而在南方游历。

谊的愉悦也激发了杜甫写作的灵感。

杜甫的作品深受社会动荡的影响。安禄山叛乱震动中国时，杜甫已经四十四岁了。[1] 反叛者占领都城后，杜甫被俘，但他逃了出来，藏在一座寺院里，这段经历深深震动了杜甫。在他后期的诗歌中，社会现实的悲惨是一个永恒的主题，杜甫也是第一个真实描写现实和社会问题的诗人。

尽管杜甫没有通过科举考试——这一事实一直让历史学家们困惑不已——但他花了几年时间试图帮助政府重建秩序，不过却彻底失败了。在他的余生中，杜甫从未真正安定下来，也从未停止为山河动荡而痛苦。杜甫的诗歌充满了无处安放的漂泊，他让我们从一个流亡者的视角来看待战争给人类造成的巨大的苦难。他站在无边的绝望中，敏锐地感知着逃离战争的难民的痛苦和希望。

———————————

杜甫出生在中国北方的洛阳附近，刚出生不久他的母亲就去世了。他的诗中经常提到几个同父异母的兄弟姐妹，却从未提到他的继母。如前所述，在公元 735 年，杜甫参加了科举考试却落榜了，这一事实一直让学者们感到十分困惑，也许是因为杜甫的写作风格太超前了，考官们根本无法完全理解。公元 744 年，杜甫遇到了李白，这位年长的诗人对杜甫产生了巨大的影响，一部分原因是年龄的差异，但也因为李白的生活方式与古典的诗人隐士的理想颇为接近。两年后，杜甫搬到京城，试图恢复他的官场生涯，并在公元 747 年再次参加了科举考试，但这一次，所有应试者都失败了，因为丞相

———————————

1　根据中国的年龄算法。

醉心于阻止对手在做官之路上步步高升。

不久之后杜甫成家了，并生了五个孩子。如前所述，公
元755年，安禄山叛乱爆发后，民生崩溃，杜甫的生活发生了
天翻地覆的变化。他被俘并被带回落入叛军手中的长安，与
家人分离，可能又在这时感染了疟疾。不过因为杜甫地位太
低，也并非什么重要人物，所以他幸免于难。杜甫与家人团
聚后，一场大洪水带来的饥荒让他不得不再次迁居。这个时
候，杜甫最小的孩子不幸夭折，尽管他很痛苦，但他从不自
怜，反而经常对身边人的困境和苦难感到同情：

"抚迹犹酸辛，

平人固骚屑"。

不久之后，杜甫被派到华州[1]当个小官，但他却不甚喜欢：

"束带发狂欲大叫，

簿书何急来相仍"。

公元759年，杜甫来到四川成都，在远离战火的温暖气候
中度过了五年。尽管日子拮据，但这似乎是杜甫人生中一段
快乐而高产的时光，杜甫这一时期的许多诗歌都展现了他平
静的"草堂"生活。公元762年冬天，皇帝收复了杜甫的出生
地洛阳，杜甫扬帆起航，沿着长江而下，希望重归故土。因
为他的健康状况不太好，一行人走得很慢，并在一个叫白帝
城的地方停留了两年。短短两年中，杜甫以他特有的密集写
作风格创作了四百首诗。随后他们再次出发前往洛阳，但杜
甫却在湖南去世了，终年五十八岁。

1　杜甫在陕西华州期间遇到了石壕吏，并写成《石壕吏》一诗，见第136页。

白居易

安禄山叛乱后，唐朝进入了第二个阶段，虽然这个阶段社会有所稳定，但却一直饱受战争的困扰。这一时期的主要人物是白居易（772—846）。白居易出生在一个地位不高，但受过良好教育的家庭，一家人生活在贫困的边缘。通过科举考试后，白居易在三十六岁时成了皇帝的谏臣。尽管人到中年，声名渐起，但白居易从未忘记自己早年的贫困生活。他常常直言不讳地支持那些在贫困中挣扎、背负着沉重税收的普通百姓，并对无能的官员和长期穷兵黩武强烈批判。[1] 随着白居易的诗越来越受欢迎，这些诗在普通民众中掀起了一波促进社会正义的热情，从而在朝廷上引起了保守派的愤怒。白居易随之被贬，便放弃了这种诗歌风格，继续做一个普通小官，一直到公元832年卸任。白居易的晚年生活是在中国北方的一所修葺一新的寺院里度过的，他在那里组织和编纂他毕生的作品。

白居易也叫白乐天，"乐天"的意思是快乐和幸运。白居易出生在西北，一生都是虔诚的佛教徒。

白居易很小的时候就搬到了河南，他的父亲是二品地方

1　当我读到白居易关于长期穷兵黩武的诗句，我不禁想到在他一千多年后的艾森豪威尔离开白宫前的告别演讲，他告诫说美国有"庞大的军事组织和武器行业"，在"每一个城市、每一个州议会和联邦政府的每一个办公室都能感觉到它们的影响力，包括经济、政治、甚至精神上的。我们必须"，他继续说，"防止（庞大的军事组织）获得毫无根据的影响力，无论是他们有意寻求还是无意获得的。因权力错位而造成的灾难仍然可能存在，并将持续下去。"

官的助理，所以白家虽然很穷，但很有学问。公元800年，白居易通过了科举考试。但是此后不久，因为父亲去世白居易不得不服丧两年，他的事业便中断了，遂隐退到渭河岸边。服丧给白居易的仕途造成极大不便，很快他的母亲也去世了，所以他又要为母亲丁忧几年。当白居易最终重返朝廷时，又因为写了几首诗讽刺高官的贪婪，并将其与普通百姓的苦难进行对比而失宠。白居易的敌人用他的诗歌指责他不孝，对于儒家世道而言，不孝是很严重的指控，是大不敬。这是因为白居易的母亲在看花的时候不小心坠井而死，而他却写过一些咏花之作。结果，他遭到朝廷贬谪，被派往四川一个十分偏远的地方担任长官。[1] 公元819年，白居易被召回都城，却发现尽管国家风雨飘摇，新帝却只顾大肆享乐，成天大吃大喝。他在写了讽谏之论后，又一次被流放，去了杭州任刺史。在那里，白居易修复了西湖的堤坝，极大地改善了老百姓的生活。公元825年，五十三岁的白居易被任命为苏州刺史，但他不久就病倒了。他的余生，名义上是在洛阳附近任职，但实际上是处于退休状态，整理自己的作品集，一直到公元846年去世，并留下了简单安葬的指示。白居易的圆形墓地仍然坐落在伊河岸边，上面简单地写着"白居易"。

白居易生前并非没有非议，一位诗人曾经写道：

> "让我颇为困扰的是……我们读过白居易的诗歌……他的诗感性得一塌糊涂，根本不合常规。除了有成熟雅量和深谙古典礼仪的绅士外，许多人都被这些诗给

1　白居易在四川建了一个花园，见第242页的诗。

毁了。这些诗歌在民间大肆流传，被镌刻在墙上，被母亲和父亲口口相传，用来教导自己的儿女。不论寒冬炎夏，诗中那些令人生厌、熟烂于心的言辞早已融入了人们的骨肉，无法洗去。然而在这件事上，我既没有立场，也不能用律法来控制他们。”

这倒是一段很值得为之奋斗的墓志铭了。

梅尧臣

我们要说的第一个宋代诗人是梅尧臣（1002—1060）。据说他仪表堂堂，浓眉大耳，颇有教养。梅尧臣以其固有的朴实简单而著称，即他自创的“平淡”风格，平淡的意思是“淡薄”或“无味”，强调质朴和轻描淡写而不是炫耀的装饰。梅尧臣按照经验“顺其自然”，而不是试图从中提取情感或哲学意义。他避开了“为艺术而艺术”的浮躁和夸张，有意写一些传统上来看并不值得写作的题材，例如对小儿女的关爱。梅尧臣的这一行为挑战了传统观点，即认为一些想法是崇高的，而另外一些则是平庸的，这一点使他超越了价值评判的限制，不再在有没有价值之间进行选择。

梅尧臣出生在安徽省中部一个贫困的农民家庭。十六岁的时候，因为家里太穷付不起学费，梅尧臣便跟随叔父一起去了北方的主要城市洛阳。正是在洛阳，梅尧臣得以遇见志同道合的诗友并加入了一场新的诗歌运动，该运动倡导文学应该反映日常生活而不应当由当时流行的浮夸的浪漫歌谣组成。因此，梅尧臣的许多诗歌都是以他所称的“平淡口吻”

来描绘日常生活。

在安徽建德县任低级官员的时候，梅尧臣因富有同情心而颇有声望。他愿意和"烧瓦匠与贫妇"交谈，以了解他们困苦生活中的烦恼和悲伤。史料记载，他亲自监督洪水救援工作，并努力控制当地山坡上的野火。梅尧臣还深受当地人民的爱戴，因为他用土墙代替了县城周围破败的竹篱，而以往的官员为了不这么做而不断找借口，而且可能还挪用了公款，这谁知道呢？在他离开后，人们为表达他们的感激之情，把县城的名字改成了梅城，这个名字沿用至今。公元1051年，在仁宗时期，梅尧臣终于在四十九岁时通过了最高一级的科举考试。梅尧臣留下了三千多首诗，调调古怪得出奇，他谦虚地称其为"平淡"，意为"平凡而宁静"。

苏轼

接下来是大文豪苏轼（1037—1101）。苏轼，又名苏东坡，虽然出生在一个普通家庭，但苏轼却通过最高级别的科举考试走向了仕途高位，直到因直言不讳地抨击朝廷如火如荼的变法而获罪。在著名的"乌台诗案"中，苏轼被指控背叛朝廷，亦可见于《宋刑统》第122条"愚弄朝廷妄自尊大"，最终苏轼被判有罪，并被流放到中国中部一个偏远之地，成为政府压制言论自由的早期受害者之一。但伟大的创造力往往诞生于严峻的挫折和困难之中，苦难撕裂了苏轼的生活，但似乎却激励了他的创作。他相继经历了所深爱的两个妻子的离世，更令人心碎的是他的第四个儿子在襁褓中夭折了。[1]

1　我想写这本书的一个主要原因是，我看到翻译大家王红公的书中苏轼写的关于他幼子夭折的诗时，被深深震动了。失去孩子无疑是人生中最痛苦的经历之一，而苏轼则以一种尤为强烈的方式描写了这番经历，回想

后来，他再次被流放，更因无力解决社会问题而饱受折磨。苏轼的诗歌对我们的生活很有帮助，因为他找到了面对困难和失意时所需要的平衡心态。尽管困难重重，他还是获得了超然的宁静，甚至是怀抱着一颗洒脱的心，因为他早已看透自己所经历的困难不过是宇宙演变的命运的一部分。

苏轼生于北宋时期西南部的四川省。他是一位博学大师，既是作家、诗人，又是美食家、药理学家、书法家和政治家。苏轼的弟弟和父亲也都是著名的文人，而他则在很年轻的时候便通过了最高一级的科举考试，一下引起了皇帝的注意。他更是在一次即兴创作诗歌的考试中表现出色，一举成名。二十年来，苏轼在全国各地担任过各式各样的官职，特别是在杭州任职的时候，他在西湖岸边修建了一条堤道，这条堤道现在仍在使用并以他的名字命名。公元 1078 年，苏轼写了一篇关于徐州当地制铁业问题的文章，后来又作了一篇批判王安石的文章。王安石是诗人也是苏轼的政治劲敌，本书后文亦收录了王安石的作品。结果，苏轼因此被指控背叛朝廷，经过四个月的证据收集，监察机构认定他有罪，但将死刑减为流放。苏轼因此失

（接上页）了孩子的种种，例如孩子的样子和他用的东西，这实在让人无法承受。王红公翻译了这首诗的第二部分，而我想知道苏轼是如何描述他的妻子，一个被打击摧毁的母亲的感受。由于中国诗歌不含代词，所以我不知道他写的这一打击是对"我"还是"我们"。我坚持不懈地搜寻，终于找到了整首诗的原作。令我欣慰的是，我看到苏轼对他悲痛欲绝的妻子表达了深切的同情，明确提到了她，而不是用一个性别不明的代词来指代。"母哭不可闻"，他写道，意思是"我实在不忍心听到孩子母亲的哭泣"，或者是"孩子母亲的啜泣不大能听清"。我还看到他把这场灾祸归咎于自己身上，而不是指责孩子的母亲。我一遍又一遍地重温这首诗。见第 128 页。

势，并被贬谪到了长江边上的偏远小镇湖北黄州，过着没有薪俸的贫困生活。在一位朋友的帮助下，他在"东坡"上建了一间小屋，并因此自称东坡，开始了佛教冥想。正是在黄州的时候，苏轼创作了他最著名的几首诗和几幅书法作品，记录了他在寒食节时孤独凄凉的状态。[1] 公元1086年，苏轼被新朝廷召回，但最终在公元1094年被流放到更加偏远的南方城市惠州。苏轼结过三次婚，但是他的妻子都在他有生之年去世了。和当时大多数官员一样，苏轼不得不常常与家人分离。而面对妻子相继离世，他悲痛欲绝，写了很多感人的悼亡诗。苏轼去世后，他的弟弟将他安葬在他的第二任妻子旁边。苏轼在晚年时期成为了素食主义者，他写道：

> "自下狱后，念己亲经患难，不异鸡鸭之在庖厨，不欲使有生之类，受无量怖苦，遂断杀。"

从当代的视角来看，苏轼一生中的关键时刻"乌台诗案"可以看作是一场争取言论自由的斗争。朝廷的不利裁决压制了异议，毫不夸张地说，这一裁决对近一千年后的中国社会仍然有影响。

李清照

李清照（1084—约1151）出生于中国东部沿海现今山东省的一个士大夫之家，从小受到与家中男孩子同等的待遇。她的父亲是苏轼的学生，所以她从小便在博学的氛围中

1　见第148页。

长大。早在公元 1101 年她出嫁之前，她的诗就已经家喻户晓了。李清照似乎有一段幸福的婚姻，她的丈夫和她一样有着开明的观点[1]，尽管丈夫因为做官常常需要外出，但他们共享着思想上的自由，有很多共同的艺术爱好，并收藏了大量的书籍、绘画、书法、古董和雕刻品。他们都热爱诗歌，经常为对方写诗。公元 1127 年，北宋落入金人手中，他们的房子也被烧毁了。李清照逃往南方的南京，带着剩余的家产和她的丈夫在那里会合。然而，在这场混乱中，李清照的丈夫在两年后便去世了，这重重打击了李清照，以至于她从未完全恢复。

在四十五岁左右，李清照发现自己在歧视女性的宋朝社会失去了庇护，她的丈夫、父亲和兄弟都去世了，她收藏的大量艺术品也散落各地。人们对她晚年的二十年知之甚少，但她后期的诗歌透着一种忧郁和对战争的仇恨，这与她年轻时陷入爱河时所作的早期诗歌形成了鲜明的对比。[2]野史记载，李清照的第二段婚姻中，她的丈夫待她很不好，因此她便与他离婚了。为避开闲言碎语，她在杭州过着相对贫困的生活。李清照创作了大量的作品，包括十三本诗集里的一千多首诗，还有一本散文集，但是只有大约五十首诗流传了下来，不过这些足以巩固她在世界诗坛的地位。

在中国，诗歌几乎是男性独有的传统，因此李清照值得

1　最近有人对此提出质疑。

2　第 190 页的《如梦令·常记溪亭日暮》是李清照年轻时写的，第 142 页的《鹧鸪天·寒日萧萧上琐窗》是她年老时写的，对比两首词能清楚地看到这一点。

特别关注。尽管历史上曾有过许多女诗人，但她们的作品很少能够流传至今。女性一般都受过教育，但从很小的时候开始，她们便被束之闺阁，这不可避免地阻碍了她们的想象力，也使她们无法享受男性认为理所当然的知识和艺术自由。尽管也有一些例外，有些家庭把女孩跟男孩一样看待，但更值得一提的是一些女性在摆脱社会束缚时表现出的足智多谋。宋朝的婚姻通常是家庭之间的一种商业安排——当然也有明显的例外——而不是像我们当今社会的理想那样，是独一无二而且是建立在浪漫爱情之上。在当时，女性能够与已婚男性建立起一种我们所谓的"浪漫"关系，也就是说，这些关系发乎于情而非出于经济或政治利益。在那个年代，男人纳妾或与妓女有染是完全正常的。这些女人的吸引力不仅在于她们的外表，还在于她们的智慧，她们的谈吐和艺术造诣，而通过这种方式，她们能够获得经济上的独立。因此，她们也获得了精神上的独立。有证据表明，女性创作了大量的诗歌，但多数都没有保存下来。值得庆幸的是，李清照的诗歌是幸存下来的传统的一部分，她的诗歌真是耀眼夺目，熠熠生辉，我希望你也这么认为。

但是奇怪的是，李清照的名字被国际天文学联合会（行星系统命名工作组）用来代表两个撞击坑，一个是小行星撞击水星南半球形成的，另一个则是小行星撞击金星北半球形成的。对此我真的百思不得其解，也忍不住想知道她若是知道了会怎么想。

陆游

最后，在陆游（1125—1210）的陪伴下我们即将抵达终

点。宋朝北部沦陷，都城南迁至杭州的时候，陆游才几个月大。在八岁之前，陆游一直在乱世中逃难，过着贫困的难民生活，直到在祖辈在南方的农场安顿下来。陆游通过了科举考试，作为一名官员，他极力主张与北方入侵者进行军事对抗。因此，他与主和派为主导的朝廷发生了冲突。陆游对自己的事业产生了强烈的挫败感，开始以某种刻意的狂野和豪放来行事，并自号"放翁"。他四处游历，辗转担任数个小官职，多次因不负责任的任性行为而被撤职。陆游的诗歌涉猎广泛，富有想象力。在六十四岁卸任之后，他回到了小时候住过的农场，并忍受着日益贫困的生活。在人生最后的二十年里，陆游每天都会写一首诗。他的作品更像是笔记或日志，详细记录了乡村生活的点滴、季节变化以及在人生不同时期人们对生活的不同关注点。

十月十七日一个雨天的清晨，陆游出生在渭河上一艘漂浮的小船里。在他的一生中，大宋王朝历经分裂，时而面临着来自北方的入侵威胁。陆游八十六岁时去世，他声称自己身体康健得益于常食珍珠大麦和木耳的饮食习惯。陆游留下了一大批作品，多达一万一千多首诗。

十二岁时，陆游已经是一位优秀的作家，对战略很感兴趣，就像李白一样，陆游也成为了一位卓越的剑客。他十九岁时参加科举考试，但没有通过。十年后，他成为了所在地区最优秀的书生，却因为遭到一位无能官员的嫉恨而无法更进一步。直到这个官员死后，陆游才得以进入仕途。

陆游和他的表妹唐婉一起长大，情投意合，二十岁的时候两人结婚了，但没有孩子。陆游的母亲不喜欢他的妻子，

最后硬逼着陆游休妻。[1] 八年后，陆游偶然遇见唐婉和她的新丈夫一起坐在一个花园中。唐婉看见陆游，便端着一杯酒走了过来。当她把酒递给他的时候，陆游看到她的眼睛里充满了泪水。他一饮而尽咽下那杯苦酒，心如刀绞。陆游在去世前一年，也就是他八十五岁的时候，写了一首名为《沈园》的诗，来纪念唐婉和那个近五十年前她给他送酒的地方。他们的爱情故事在中国家喻户晓。

公元 1172 年，陆游正式开始了他的军旅生涯，担任军事参谋。这使他有机会实现他毕生的梦想——看到中国再次统一，这种爱国主义在他的许多诗中都有所体现。然而，当时的宋朝腐败而懒散，他并没有机会充分发挥自己的才能。陆游觉得自己在朝堂上没有立足之地，开始放纵自己，沉溺在酗酒之中，来忘却自己个人生活和事业上的不得志。虽然陆游自称"放翁"，但他在诗中多有自嘲。经历了几次晋升和贬谪后，陆游于公元 1190 年卸任归田，隐居在农村老家。在那里陆游度过了生命的最后二十年，直到公元 1210 年 1 月 26 日去世。

1　他为什么就不能说"不！"？

十一　如果、也许和可能

　　我忠实的朋友们，那些坚持不懈地追随这个旅程的人们，你们在中国历史的大片中穿梭，在亚原子粒子的严峻图景中奋力挣扎，只为了体验：

上 | 下 | 奇 | 魅 | 美 | 真

　　我终于可以确定地说，我说到正题了。

　　我想拿一台大型强子对撞机到这七十首中国诗歌面前，把他们撞开，看看里面到底是什么。我将把汉字散落开来，这样我们就可以看看它们噼里啪啦穿越时空的轨迹。我并没有单独呈现单个标本，而是试图以一种当代的声音将它们结合在一起——至少，我已经尽力把它们放在更广阔的背景中了。

　　在我将这些诗歌分为六类的时候，我仿佛看到某种模式从云雾中浮现出来。在我看来，前三个夸克的名字意味着由斗争而生的情感。"上"让人联想到这样一幅画面：诗人醉醺醺地欢呼着，一杯接一杯沉醉在醉酒的兴奋与癫狂中，他们欢快地舞动着，越过天才与疯子之间的界线；"下"指的是与悲伤的斗争，这种悲伤是自然的残酷和人性的残忍造成的；而"奇"指的是对未知或无法解释的事物的恐惧，是与大自然最古怪的形式的斗争，比如秋天的大风、蛆虫、老鼠

Translation of Introduction　前言译文

和蝗虫。诗人似乎通过用古典诗歌严苛的结构来展现世界的丑陋和让人难受的一面来嘲弄我们，嘲笑我们相信僧侣和先知可以告诉我们躲避人类命运的方法。后三个夸克的名字"魅""美"和"真"似乎是指人与他人、与自然、与整个社会的关系。"魅"指的是友谊和家庭的纽带，"美"指的是与自然和谐共处所带来的平和与舒适，而"真"则呈现了不可避免的现实，这种现实将个体联系在一起，并赋予我们对整个社会的责任。我们每个人都可以自行决定一首诗属于六个夸克类别中的哪一个，对你来说，哪些是"上"，哪些充满"魅"，而哪些不得不归于"奇"中呢？

最后，我希望当我们凝视这些诗句的时候，都能退后一步，共享人性的共通之处，因为它们从其所在的遥远时空和时代背景与我们的生活遥相呼应。如果我们能瞥见这些千年前的人的思想，并从中找到共鸣，那么也许，在现今这个似乎比以往任何时候都更难以驾驭的世界里，我们可能会发现，我们的共识远远多于分歧。

祈立天
认命斋
惊蛰，2021